The Law God Didn't Write

Why Modern States Should Abolish the Ḥudūd Punishments

Mark A. Gabriel, PhD

Gabriel Press

This book is a scholarly examination of Islamic criminal-law doctrine, juristic interpretation, and the limits of coercive authority in the modern state. It does not attribute one uniform position to all Muslim jurists, communities, or states.

First edition, 2026

Published by Gabriel Press

Paperback ISBN: 979-8-9972753-3-4

eBook ISBN: 979-8-9972753-7-2

Library of Congress Control Number: 2026920911

Printed in the United States of America

Abstract

This book examines one of the most controversial areas of Islamic criminal law: the punishments traditionally associated with theft, adultery, false accusation, alcohol use, armed violence, rebellion, and leaving Islam. These punishments are often described as fixed by God and therefore beyond human change, but this study argues that the matter is far more complicated. Using the work of the Egyptian legal scholar Aḫmad Fatḫī Bahnasi as a central source, the book shows that these punishments do not operate automatically. Before any punishment can be enforced, human beings must decide what the offense means, what evidence is sufficient, what exceptions apply, who may be punished, and which legal opinion should be followed. Muslim jurists themselves disagreed on many of these questions, which means that the law reaching the courtroom is shaped by interpretation, selection, and human judgment. This is the meaning behind the title, *The Law God Didn't Write*. The book does not argue that Islam has no moral teachings about crime or wrongdoing. Rather, it argues that God did not hand modern governments a complete criminal code containing all the definitions, procedures, exceptions, and punishments that states today claim to enforce in His name. The book also asks whether modern states should still have the power to impose punishments such as amputation, flogging, stoning, crucifixion, or death for changing one's religion, and it concludes that they should not. Modern governments possess far greater power than rulers in the classical period, including national police forces, prisons, surveillance systems, digital records, forensic technology, and centralized bureaucracies. Giving such institutions sacred authority over the body and conscience creates serious dangers. The book therefore moves beyond the idea that these punishments can simply be reformed through better procedures. Fair trials and strong safeguards are necessary, but they cannot make mutilation proportionate, stoning humane, or forced belief genuine. Modern states should abolish these punishments. This does not mean abandoning the moral concerns behind them. Property can be protected without cutting off a hand, families can be strengthened without stoning, public safety can be defended without crucifixion, reputation can be protected without flogging, and religious faith can be taught and preserved without executing those who leave it. The central argument of this book is simple: moral values can be preserved without preserving the violence once used to enforce them.

Table of Contents

Introduction

From Reforming the Ḥudūd to Questioning Their Place in the Modern State

For much of the modern debate over Islamic criminal law, the central question has been framed in reformist terms. Scholars have asked whether the classical ḥudūd can be reconciled with constitutional safeguards, modern evidentiary standards, judicial independence, proportionality, and international human-rights law. Within that framework, the underlying institution is generally preserved. The work of reform is directed toward restricting its application, raising the threshold of proof, limiting executive interference, selecting less severe juristic opinions, or postponing enforcement until certain social, economic, and political conditions have been met. The assumption is that the punishments may remain part of the law if the path leading to them can be made sufficiently careful, just, and restrained. [1]

That was also the direction of my own earlier scholarly work. In my doctoral research on Islamic criminal law and international human-rights law, I examined whether the enforcement of ḥudūd ordinances might be brought within constitutional and procedural safeguards. My purpose was never to defend arbitrary punishment or to reproduce the classical system without criticism. I sought a legal path through which deeply rooted Islamic doctrines might be reconciled with due process, equality, judicial accountability, and human dignity. That reformist undertaking remains important. It exposed the dangers created by weak evidence, coerced confession, discriminatory rules, political interference, and irreversible punishment. It also demonstrated that the invocation of Islamic law cannot itself establish justice. The character of the state, the independence of the judiciary, the protection of the

1For a representative formulation of this reformist approach in the author's earlier work, see Mark A. Gabriel, 'Reforming Hudud Ordinances to Reconcile Islamic Criminal Law with International Human Rights Law' (PhD diss., University of Cape Town, 2016), 17–18, 160–62.

accused, and the social conditions in which punishment occurs are all part of the moral and constitutional inquiry. [2]

Yet the more closely the ḥudūd are examined, the more difficult it becomes to remain within the reformist question alone. A deeper question gradually emerges. The decisive issue may no longer be how the modern state can reform these punishments, but whether any modern government should claim the authority to enforce them at all. This study grows from that intellectual development. It does not begin from hostility toward Islamic jurisprudence, nor from the assumption that the classical jurists lacked seriousness, moral concern, or legal sophistication. The tradition contains extensive reasoning about culpability, doubt, necessity, coercion, testimony, confession, repentance, jurisdiction, ownership, public welfare, and the avoidance of wrongful punishment. In many places the jurists sought to restrain rulers, narrow liability, and distinguish between degrees of responsibility. Their work deserves accurate reconstruction before it is subjected to criticism.

Nor does this study deny the continuing importance of the moral concerns historically associated with the ḥudūd. Every functioning society must protect life, property, reputation, family responsibility, public safety, and accountability. Theft remains wrong. Murder and organized violence require a serious legal response. Sexual exploitation, malicious accusation, public disorder, and conduct that endangers others cannot simply be ignored. The question is not whether these values should disappear. The question is whether their protection requires the preservation of corporal, capital, political, and conscience-based punishments developed within a premodern legal order.

Bahnasi's Book as the Point of Departure

Aḥmad Fatḥī Bahnasi's Al-Ḥudūd fī al-Islām provides an especially revealing text through which to examine this question. Bahnasi was not merely collecting historical opinions. His book belongs to a wider

---

2Gabriel, 'Reforming Hudud Ordinances,' 17–20, 160–61, 197, 209. The dissertation distinguished Shariah from human jurisprudence, employed necessity, reality, and doubt as reform instruments, and proposed alternative punishments compatible with human-rights standards.

modern project seeking the restoration of Islamic jurisprudence as an alternative to legal systems described as foreign or imported. He presents the inherited legal tradition as capable of responding to every time and place and as a legitimate foundation for contemporary legislation. His work therefore stands at the meeting point of classical doctrine and modern political aspiration. It allows us to observe how a juristic system formed over centuries is translated into a program for the modern state. [3]

Bahnasi's method is systematic. He begins with a general theory of punishment and then locates the ḥudūd within the wider structure of Islamic criminal jurisprudence. He distinguishes them from qiṣāṣ, diyya, and taʿzīr before moving through theft, ḥirāba, unlawful sexual intercourse, false accusation, drinking and intoxication, rebellion, and apostasy. Throughout the work he records important disagreements among the schools concerning the definition of offenses, evidentiary requirements, legal capacity, ownership, protected status, punishment, and enforcement. Those disagreements are not secondary to the present argument. They are central to it, because they reveal how much human reasoning is required before a punishment described as fixed can become operative law. [4]

Bahnasi classifies the ḥudūd as punishments determined by the lawgiver and generally connected to the rights of God. That classification carries major legal consequences. A punishment understood as a divine right is not treated like ordinary legislation. It is not readily subject to pardon, settlement, reduction, or revision. Once the offense has been established under the required conditions, the ruler or authorized authority is expected to enforce the prescribed consequence. Yet the description of the punishment as fixed does not remove the human judgment required before the state can impose it. The law must still determine the elements of the offense, the status of

---

3Aḥmad Fatḥī Bahnasi, al-Ḥudūd fī al-Islām (Alexandria: Muʾassasat Shabāb al-Jāmiʿa, n.d.), 3–6. Bahnasi's introduction contrasts Islamic jurisprudence with imported legislation and presents the inherited tradition as capable of renewed development and contemporary codification.

4Bahnasi, al-Ḥudūd fī al-Islām, 3–6, 29–39. Bahnasi first sets out a general theory of punishment, then classifies ḥudūd, qiṣāṣ, diyya, and taʿzīr before treating the individual offenses.

the accused, the admissibility of evidence, the existence of doubt, the legal effect of repentance, and the identity of the authority entitled to act. [5]

Theft illustrates the difficulty. The Qur'anic command does not independently settle the minimum value, the meaning of protected custody, the nature of ownership, the effect of debt, access within the family, the treatment of public property, necessity, common ownership, or the physical and commercial character of the object taken. Similar problems appear throughout the other offenses. Jurists disagree over which intoxicants fall within the category of khamr, whether punishment depends upon consumption or actual intoxication, and whether forty or eighty lashes constitute the proper sanction. They disagree over the conditions of iḥṣān, the number and retraction of confessions, the relationship between flogging and stoning, the meaning of the reported verse of stoning, and the boundaries of ḥirāba, rebellion, and apostasy. These disagreements do not concern peripheral details. They determine whether a person is acquitted, punished discretionarily, flogged, amputated, crucified, or executed. [6]

The central difficulty can therefore be stated plainly: the punishment is presented as fixed, while the legal path leading to it is constructed through contested human interpretation. That contradiction becomes more serious because the penalties are irreversible. A mistaken fine may be repaid. An unjust prison sentence, although profoundly harmful, may at least be terminated and compensated in part. A severed hand cannot be restored. A person killed by stoning, crucifixion, or execution cannot be returned to life when new evidence appears or a legal interpretation changes.

Procedure, Severity, and the Modern State

The classical juristic tradition responded to this danger through procedural restraint. Bahnasi repeatedly discusses the avoidance of the

5Bahnasi, al-Ḥudūd fī al-Islām, 30–39. His legal definition of a ḥadd joins three propositions: determination of the punishment, obligatory enforcement, and attribution to the right of God.

6Bahnasi, al-Ḥudūd fī al-Islām, 61–90, 99–162. The detailed chapters record disagreement concerning theft, ḥirāba, zinā, qadhf, drinking, rebellion, and apostasy.

ḥudūd through doubt, the discouragement of confession, the possibility of retracting an admission, demanding witness requirements, concealment of private wrongdoing, and limitations upon judicial knowledge. These doctrines certainly demonstrate an awareness of the danger of wrongful punishment. Yet they also reveal an internal tension. The substantive law declares the punishment fixed and mandatory, while the procedural law searches for reasons not to impose it. In effect, procedure repeatedly attempts to rescue the accused from the consequences of the substantive rule. [7]

This tension acquires a different meaning when the law is placed in the hands of the modern state. Classical jurists did not operate within the institutional world of contemporary government. Modern authorities possess centralized police power, professional prosecution, intelligence services, prisons, digital surveillance, forensic laboratories, biometric records, administrative databases, and the capacity to impose one selected interpretation as binding law upon millions of citizens. These powers can weaken the practical restraints that once made certain offenses exceptionally difficult to prove. A rule developed in an environment where private conduct was difficult to investigate may become far more dangerous when enforced by a surveillance-capable state. Broad categories such as corruption in the land, rebellion, and apostasy may also be directed against political opposition, theological dissent, academic inquiry, conversion, or criticism of religious authority. [8]

The modern state is not the classical imamate. It may be democratic or authoritarian, constitutional or arbitrary, stable or corrupt. It may be controlled by a monarchy, military establishment, political party, religious institution, or revolutionary movement. It may also be

---

7Bahnasi, al-Ḥudūd fī al-Islām, 20–29, 61–90, 99–139. His discussion includes doubt, confession, witness restrictions, necessity, concealment, repentance, and other doctrines that may prevent or delay enforcement.

8On the structural difference between classical juristic governance and the centralized modern state, see Wael B. Hallaq, Shariʿa: Theory, Practice, Transformations (Cambridge: Cambridge University Press, 2009), 355–500; and Hallaq, The Impossible State: Islam, Politics, and Modernity's Moral Predicament (New York: Columbia University Press, 2013), 45–112.

displaced by an armed organization that declares itself an Islamic state and claims authority to administer Islamic criminal law. None of these actors should be permitted to avoid scrutiny by presenting its own coercive judgment as the direct enforcement of God's right. The attribution of punishment to God does not necessarily restrain political power. It may instead shield that power from moral and constitutional accountability.

A citizen may challenge an ordinary statute as unjust, disproportionate, discriminatory, or unconstitutional. When the same punishment is presented as divine law, criticism may itself be treated as irreligious, rebellious, or hostile to Islam. The authority then acquires not only the power to punish, but also the power to sanctify its own interpretation. This is the constitutional danger at the heart of the present study. The state, regime, or armed movement selects among disputed human interpretations and then presents the result as though its own political responsibility has disappeared.

From Procedural Reform to Substantive Transformation

The difficulty is compounded by the hierarchical legal order reflected in many of the classical doctrines recorded by Bahnasi. The rules distinguish among Muslims and non-Muslims, free and enslaved persons, men and women, married and unmarried persons, chaste and unchaste persons, residents and outsiders, and persons possessing different levels of testimonial or legal capacity. These distinctions developed within a premodern social and political structure. They cannot simply be removed from their historical setting while the punishments are preserved unchanged, because criminal doctrine and legal status developed together. A modern constitutional order, by contrast, must begin from equal legal personhood. Responsibility and protection should not depend upon religion, sex, inherited status, or prior moral reputation. [9]

The issue is therefore broader than the physical severity of individual punishments. It concerns the legal and political order to which those punishments belong. Bahnasi's defense of the ḥudūd rests

9Bahnasi, al-Ḥudūd fī al-Islām, 20–39, 99–139. The rules he records distinguish legal consequences by religion, freedom status, sex, marital history, chastity, and testimonial capacity.

upon an unsustainable transfer of authority from revelation and classical juristic interpretation to modern political institutions. The phrase "right of God" does not prove that every rule placed within that category was directly and immutably prescribed by God. It is itself a juristic classification developed through human legal reasoning. Bahnasi's own presentation shows that the operative system depends upon interpretation, analogy, custom, political judgment, social status, and disagreement among schools. A legislature that selects one threshold, one evidentiary rule, one definition, or one punishment is not merely transmitting a complete divine code. It is choosing among competing human constructions and must accept responsibility for that choice. [10]

The title The Law God Didn't Write should therefore be understood with precision. It does not deny that the Qur'an and the Prophetic tradition contain moral teachings, legal principles, or particular penal references. It makes a narrower and more consequential claim: the complete criminal code later enforced in the name of the ḥudūd—with its definitions, thresholds, status distinctions, evidentiary rules, exceptions, and institutional procedures—was not written by God as one self-executing statute. It was assembled through human jurisprudence and becomes positive law only when human authorities select, codify, interpret, and enforce it.

This critique does not depend solely upon contemporary human-rights instruments, although those instruments remain important. Nor does it rest only upon the observation that the punishments appear harsh to modern readers. It arises from the internal structure of the legal tradition described by Bahnasi himself. The offenses are extensively disputed, the evidence is fallible, the punishments are irreversible, the social classifications are unequal, the ruler's authority is assumed rather than constitutionally demonstrated, and the procedural rules repeatedly seek to avoid enforcement. At the same time, the modern state possesses coercive powers far exceeding those of the political order in which the doctrines developed.

Taken together, these considerations lead beyond procedural reform. A higher evidentiary threshold cannot make an intrinsically

---

10For an earlier formulation of the distinction between divine Shariah and fallible juristic law, see Gabriel, 'Reforming Hudud Ordinances,' 19–20. See also Mohammad Hashim Kamali, Shariʿah Law: An Introduction (Oxford: Oneworld, 2008), 14–28.

disproportionate punishment proportionate. Judicial independence cannot make execution for peaceful religious conversion compatible with freedom of conscience. A moratorium does not answer whether the state should possess the power after the moratorium ends. Selecting the most merciful school does not resolve the broader problem of allowing government to inflict irreversible bodily punishment in the name of God. Where ḥudūd laws remain in force, procedural safeguards are urgently necessary; but procedural improvement does not settle the legitimacy of the institution itself. [11]

The position advanced in this study is therefore constructive rather than merely negative. Muslim societies can preserve the moral objectives associated with justice, accountability, protection of life and property, family responsibility, reputation, sobriety, repentance, and public safety without preserving the classical corporal and capital punishments. Theft may be addressed through restitution, compensation, proportionate sentencing, and rehabilitation. Violent crime may be punished through ordinary criminal law. Sexual violence requires a consent-centered framework that protects victims. Adultery may remain a serious religious and moral wrong without becoming a corporal or capital offense. Malicious accusation may be addressed through defamation law, compensation, retraction, and proportionate sanctions. Alcohol-related harm may be regulated through public-health measures and laws against dangerous conduct. Armed insurrection may be addressed through constitutional security law, while peaceful religious change must remain a matter of conscience.

The central thesis of this study may therefore be stated as follows:

> *The moral purposes associated with the ḥudūd may be preserved, but modern states should abolish their classical corporal, capital, political, and conscience-based punishments, and no regime or armed movement claiming the right to enforce*

11Gabriel, 'Reforming Hudud Ordinances,' 160–97, originally argued for alternative punishments and constitutional reconciliation. The present study advances beyond that position by questioning whether modern political authorities should retain the underlying power at all.

Islamic criminal law should be permitted to impose them.

The chapters that follow first reconstruct Bahnasi's legal project before subjecting it to sustained criticism. They distinguish revelation from juristic classification, examine the theory of the rights of God, analyze the individual offenses and punishments, and consider the relationship between procedure, social status, bodily injury, political authority, and conscience. The aim is not to dismiss the Islamic legal tradition, but to confront honestly the point at which historical inheritance, modern state power, and human dignity can no longer be reconciled by procedural adjustment alone.

Method and Scope

This study employs a critical doctrinal and constitutional method centered on Bahnasi's Al-Ḥudūd fī al-Islām. It reads Bahnasi as a modern juristic advocate of the classical penal tradition and examines the legal reasoning through which scriptural sources, school doctrines, evidentiary rules, status classifications, and governmental authority are joined together. The book does not claim that Bahnasi represents every Muslim jurist or every historical application of Islamic criminal law. His text is used as a disciplined primary point of departure because it records significant disagreement within the tradition while also presenting the ḥudūd as suitable for contemporary restoration. The analysis proceeds offense by offense and then brings the recurring problems together institutionally: juristic plurality, codification, unequal personhood, procedural avoidance, bodily irreversibility, political legitimacy, and freedom of conscience. The constitutional inquiry evaluates not only how a punishment is imposed but whether the conduct should be criminalized, whether the sentence is proportionate, and whether a modern state may claim sacred authority for a coercive rule selected from disputed jurisprudence. Human-rights principles are employed as standards of dignity, equality, bodily integrity, fair process, and religious freedom, while the constructive chapters distinguish the moral purposes of the tradition from the historical punishments attached to them.

Part One

Bahnasi's Legal Project and Its Foundational Assumptions

Chapter One

Aḥmad Fatḥī Bahnasi and the Restoration of Islamic Criminal Law

Aḥmad Fatḥī Bahnasi's Al-Ḥudūd fī al-Islām is not written merely as a historical survey of classical Islamic criminal jurisprudence. From its opening pages, the book advances a larger legal and political project. Bahnasi seeks to demonstrate that Islamic jurisprudence remains capable of providing a comprehensive foundation for contemporary criminal legislation and that Muslim societies should return to it rather than continue relying upon laws received from foreign legal systems. He praises the accumulated principles, rules, and juristic methods of Islamic law and contrasts them with what he describes as imported legislation that may not conform to the customs, character, and social conditions of Muslim societies. In his presentation, Islamic jurisprudence is not a historical achievement to be admired from a distance. It is a living legal system capable of development within the spirit of revelation and suitable for every time and place. [12]

The force of this opening should not be underestimated. Bahnasi is not merely arguing that Islamic jurisprudence deserves scholarly respect or that it can contribute moral principles to public life. He is presenting it as an alternative source of positive legislation. His book belongs to a broader twentieth-century effort to move Islamic criminal law from the library, mosque, and law faculty into the legislative chamber and courtroom. This restorationist purpose explains both the strength and the limitation of the work. Bahnasi's strength lies in his serious engagement with the juristic tradition. He does not reduce Islamic criminal law to slogans or isolated Qur'anic verses. He draws upon the major Sunni schools, records disagreements among jurists, and occasionally refers to positions beyond the four-school structure. He recognizes plurality as an established feature of Islamic legal reasoning and argues that contemporary legislation should not be confined mechanically to one school when other juristic opinions may better suit present circumstances.

12Bahnasi, al-Ḥudūd fī al-Islām, 3–6.

At the same time, the restorationist objective shapes the inquiry from beginning to end. Bahnasi starts from confidence in the continuing authority and suitability of the inherited system. His principal task is not to ask whether the modern state should possess the power to enforce the classical punishments. It is to explain the system, demonstrate its purposes, present its juristic details, and support its contemporary relevance. A historical study might ask how the law of ḥudūd emerged, how schools differed, how rulers applied or avoided the punishments, and how the category changed across time and place. A constitutional study might ask whether the doctrines can be reconciled with equal citizenship, freedom of conscience, proportional punishment, and the institutional character of modern government. Bahnasi begins from a different question: how may Islamic criminal jurisprudence be understood and presented as a viable legal framework for contemporary Muslim society?

Because the book begins from that position, juristic disagreement is generally treated as evidence of flexibility rather than as possible evidence against restoring the penal system itself. The existence of several opinions allows the modern legislator to select among them, and the diversity of the tradition becomes a resource for codification. Such an approach may be defensible where the disputed rule concerns an ordinary commercial, procedural, or administrative matter. It becomes far more difficult where the legislative selection determines whether a person will be flogged, amputated, crucified, or executed. In that setting, plurality does not merely provide flexibility. It places extraordinary coercive power in the hands of whichever authority decides which interpretation will become law.

The Architecture of Bahnasi's Penal Theory

Bahnasi begins not with the individual offenses, but with a general theory of punishment capable of supporting them. He defines punishment as a consequence established by the lawgiver to deter people from committing prohibited acts and abandoning required duties. Punishment operates both before and after the offense. The threatened consequence is intended to discourage the initial act, while enforcement is expected to prevent repetition and communicate the seriousness of the violation. Deterrence therefore stands near the foundation of the penal system. Punishment is not presented merely as retaliation for completed wrongdoing; it is an instrument through which law protects society, disciplines the offender, and maintains the moral order. [13]

Bahnasi also distinguishes between punishment in this world and punishment in the hereafter. The worldly sanction is administered within society, while the otherworldly consequence belongs to divine judgment. He then considers whether the enforcement of a worldly penalty may expiate the sin and protect the offender from punishment in the next life. The reports he cites support the view that legal punishment may possess a purifying effect, whereas an offense concealed from human authority may remain subject to divine judgment. This introduces a spiritual dimension into the theory. Punishment becomes not only deterrence, social protection, and correction, but also possible purification. [14]

Within Bahnasi's framework, this theological dimension gives moral meaning to severity. Bodily suffering may be described as beneficial to the offender because it is understood to cleanse the sin in this life rather than leave the person exposed to punishment in the hereafter. Yet this rationale immediately raises an institutional difficulty. A government cannot verify the spiritual effect of flogging, amputation, or execution. It cannot know whether punishment has purified the soul or whether repentance has been accepted by God. Once spiritual expiation becomes part of the justification for coercive law, the state begins to exercise authority over matters lying beyond human institutional knowledge. That criticism will be developed later. At this stage, however, it is important to understand Bahnasi's position fairly: crime is not merely a violation of public legislation, but may simultaneously constitute disobedience to God, injury to society, corruption of the offender, and a threat to temporal and eternal welfare.

Bahnasi explains that punishment possesses both an individual and a social function. The individual function seeks to influence the offender through discipline, correction, and deterrence from future wrongdoing. The social function protects the community from criminal harm and seeks either to reform the offender or, where reform is regarded as

---

13Bahnasi, al-Ḥudūd fī al-Islām, 7–20.

14Bahnasi, al-Ḥudūd fī al-Islām, 10–17. His treatment links worldly punishment with deterrence and, in certain reports, with expiation from punishment in the hereafter.

impossible, to remove or neutralize the danger. Islamic law, in his account, combines both purposes. It does not entirely disregard the offender's personality, because individual circumstances may be considered in discretionary punishment. The clearest example is taʿzīr, where the judge or ruler may respond to the offender's condition, the seriousness of the conduct, and the needs of society. Flexibility is openly acknowledged in this part of the system. [15]

The difficult question is why that flexibility disappears, or becomes sharply restricted, once conduct is classified as a ḥadd offense. Bahnasi's answer is that the lawgiver has already determined the consequence. Human authority may investigate whether the legal requirements have been satisfied, but it may not substitute a punishment it regards as more suitable. This distinction establishes the architecture of the book. Taʿzīr permits adaptation; qiṣāṣ and diyya concern injuries to individuals and may allow retaliation, compensation, or pardon; the ḥudūd are treated as fixed punishments protecting divine and public interests. The legitimacy of the entire structure therefore depends heavily upon classification. Once an offense is placed within the ḥudūd, the prescribed punishment ceases to be one possible social response and becomes the response considered to have been determined by the lawgiver. [16]

Severity, Safeguards, and the Conservative Argument

Bahnasi does not deny that some punishments are severe. His defense is more serious than denial. He argues that severity must be understood in relation to the gravity of the protected interest and the strict conditions required before punishment may be imposed. His treatment of zinā provides the clearest example. Flogging and stoning are admittedly severe, but conviction requires four witnesses testifying with exceptional precision or a valid confession. The harshness of the punishment is therefore balanced, in his reasoning, by evidentiary restrictions designed to make wrongful conviction exceedingly difficult. Theft follows the same pattern. Amputation is defended as necessary to protect property and social security, while its application is surrounded by conditions concerning value, custody, ownership, necessity, and

15Bahnasi, al-Ḥudūd fī al-Islām, 14–29.

16Bahnasi, al-Ḥudūd fī al-Islām, 30–39.

doubt. Bahnasi invokes ʿUmar's refusal to apply amputation during famine as evidence that Islamic law does not punish mechanically without regard to social conditions. [17]

In ḥirāba, the severity of execution, crucifixion, cross-amputation, or banishment is connected to the threat posed to life, travel, property, and public order. At the same time, repentance before capture may alter the legal consequences. In homicide, retaliation is presented as protection of life rather than celebration of death, while pardon and blood money introduce possibilities of mercy and social reconciliation. A recurring structure therefore appears throughout Bahnasi's defense: the punishment may seem severe when viewed alone, but its justice becomes visible when one considers the gravity of the offense, the evidentiary safeguards, the doctrines of doubt, the possibility of repentance, and the social protection expected from enforcement.

This is the strongest form of the conservative argument and it must be treated seriously. It is not enough to respond that the punishments are physically harsh. Bahnasi already knows that they are severe. He believes their severity is justified, restrained, and morally purposeful. The more difficult question is whether procedural restraint can legitimate a punishment whose nature remains disproportionate, irreversible, discriminatory, or outside the proper authority of modern government. That question cannot be answered merely by pointing again to demanding proof. A punishment may be rarely imposed and still remain unjust in the case in which it is imposed. The procedural difficulty of reaching the sentence does not itself establish the legitimacy of the sentence.

Juristic Plurality and the Problem of Modern Codification

One of the most important features of Bahnasi's work is his extensive presentation of disagreement. He does not pretend that every doctrine was unanimously settled. He records divergent positions concerning the offenses included among the ḥudūd, the number of lashes for drinking, the threshold for theft, the meaning of protected custody, the conditions of iḥṣān, the proof of unlawful sexual intercourse, the effect

---

17Bahnasi, al-Ḥudūd fī al-Islām, 61–90, 99–128. His defense repeatedly relates severity to the gravity of the protected interest and to strict conditions of proof, doubt, necessity, and repentance.

of repentance, the treatment of indirect accusation, the definition of intoxicants, and the rules governing rebellion and apostasy. He presents this plurality as evidence of the vitality and adaptability of Islamic jurisprudence. A modern Islamic code, in his view, need not be confined to one inherited school. The positions of the recognized schools and other juristic authorities may be examined for rules suited to contemporary circumstances. [18]

There is genuine intellectual openness in this method. It rejects mechanical adherence to one school and acknowledges that Islamic legal thought developed through disagreement. Yet it produces a major problem that Bahnasi does not fully confront: who chooses among the conflicting positions? In a classical setting, different judges, regions, and communities might follow different schools. A modern criminal code operates differently. The legislature generally selects one rule and makes it binding throughout the jurisdiction. It may choose one threshold for theft, one number of confessions, one understanding of stoning, one punishment for drinking, one definition of apostasy, and one theory of rebellion. Each selection is a human political decision.

Once codified, the selected interpretation acquires the force of the modern state. It is no longer simply an opinion taught in a juristic text. It is supported by police investigation, prosecution, imprisonment, corporal punishment, and execution. The choice among juristic views therefore becomes an allocation of coercive power. Bahnasi regards plurality as a means of producing an adaptable Islamic code, but the same plurality also demonstrates that the code cannot honestly be described as one complete and uncontested divine system. A statute assembled from selected Ḥanafī, Mālikī, Shāfiʿī, Ḥanbalī, Ẓāhirī, Shiʿi, and individual opinions is a new legal product. Its provisions may be inspired by Islamic jurisprudence, but the selection, combination, exclusion, and formulation belong to the modern legislature.

This distinction is essential because revelation, prophetic practice, juristic interpretation, school doctrine, analogy, custom, political administration, and codification are related but not identical forms of authority. A Qur'anic prohibition may not specify a worldly punishment. A prophetic report may be understood in more than one

---

18Bahnasi, al-Ḥudūd fī al-Islām, 3–6, 30–39, 61–162. The work records substantial disagreement while treating that plurality as a resource available to contemporary legislation.

way. A juristic rule may combine reports with analogy, customary practice, and policy. A modern statute must then choose one operative formulation. Bahnasi moves within this layered structure, but restorationist language can compress it. The final juristic system is described as Islamic law, and its contemporary adoption is presented as a return to divine legislation. The danger is that the human work of interpretation and legislation becomes hidden behind the language of restoration.

The Unresolved Authority of the Ruler

Bahnasi's penal system requires public authority. The ḥudūd are not ordinarily left to private individuals. The ruler, judge, or authorized official determines whether the conditions have been satisfied and carries out the sentence. This requirement is intended to prevent personal vengeance, disorder, and arbitrary punishment. Enforcement becomes a public function rather than a private act. Yet the modern implications are profound, because Bahnasi assumes that the ruler may inherit responsibility for enforcing the religious penal order without providing a sustained constitutional account of who that ruler is in the contemporary world. [19]

The modern authority may be a monarchy, an elected republic, a military regime, a one-party state, a revolutionary government, or a coalition between political and religious institutions. It may also be an armed organization claiming territorial rule and presenting itself as an Islamic state. Political control does not automatically establish religious legitimacy, and the capacity to enforce punishment does not establish authority to speak for God. Bahnasi's restorationist project therefore contains an unresolved institutional assumption. The classical expectation that the imam or ruler enforce the law is transferred to a modern government or quasi-state authority without a full explanation of how that authority acquires religious legitimacy, how its interpretation may be challenged, or how individuals are protected when political power presents its own selections as divine commands.

19Bahnasi, al-Ḥudūd fī al-Islām, 20–39. The penal structure presumes enforcement by the ruler, judge, or authorized public authority rather than by private individuals.

The problem becomes especially urgent in rebellion and apostasy. In those offenses the authority is not simply adjudicating a dispute between private citizens. It is deciding whether opposition to itself is religiously illegitimate and whether an individual's belief remains acceptable. The government becomes judge of its own legitimacy and guardian of the citizen's conscience. Such power cannot be justified by referring only to the classical role of the ruler, because the institutional identity of modern government is fundamentally different from the political assumptions of the classical legal order.

The purpose of this study is not to portray Bahnasi as uniquely severe or intellectually careless. His value lies precisely in the seriousness and breadth of his presentation. He represents a major line of modern Islamic legal thought: the belief that Islamic jurisprudence remains suitable for contemporary legislation, the view that inherited punishments possess continuing authority, confidence that juristic disagreement provides flexibility, the conviction that strict evidentiary conditions demonstrate mercy, and the assumption that a modern authority may act as executor of the classical penal order. Critiquing Bahnasi therefore means examining more than one book. It means examining the legal logic through which a premodern juristic tradition is transformed into a modern project of state or quasi-state enforcement.

Conclusion

Bahnasi's Al-Ḥudūd fī al-Islām presents the ḥudūd as part of a complete moral and legal order. Punishment deters wrongdoing, reforms the offender, protects society, and may contribute to spiritual expiation. Islamic jurisprudence is portrayed as rich, adaptable, and capable of supplying the foundation for contemporary law. Juristic disagreement is treated as a source of flexibility, and modern legislation may select among inherited opinions in light of social need. The internal coherence of this project depends, however, upon several assumptions: that the technical category of ḥudūd carries continuing divine authority; that a modern government or self-declared Islamic authority may inherit the enforcement role of the classical ruler; that severe punishments become just when surrounded by strict conditions; that juristic disagreement can be resolved through legislative selection; and that restoration of Islamic criminal law represents a return to divine legislation rather than the creation of a new code from selected human interpretations. [20]

The chapters that follow will examine these assumptions one by one. The first question is foundational. When Bahnasi speaks of restoring the ḥudūd as Islamic law, which elements belong directly to revelation, and which belong to the historical work of jurists, judges, rulers, customs, and schools? The distinction does not weaken the authority of revelation. It clarifies the point at which human interpretation becomes law and the point at which law acquires the coercive power to act upon the body, political freedom, and conscience. That distinction leads directly to Chapter Two, "From Divine Revelation to Juristic Classification."

20Bahnasi, al-Ḥudūd fī al-Islām, 7–39; Gabriel, 'Reforming Hudud Ordinances,' 160–97.

Chapter Two

From Divine Revelation to Juristic Classification

The restoration of Islamic criminal law depends upon a proposition that often appears self-evident but is rarely examined with sufficient precision: that the classical system of ḥudūd represents a directly revealed penal code whose essential content has already been determined by God. Once that proposition is accepted, the role of the modern legislature appears limited. The state does not seem to be creating criminal law. It appears merely to be restoring, codifying, and enforcing a law that already exists independently of human political authority. Aḥmad Fatḥī Bahnasi's treatment of the ḥudūd rests substantially upon this understanding.[21] He identifies the Qur'an as the first source of Islamic legislation and the Sunnah as the second, with the Sunnah clarifying, specifying, and completing the Qur'anic rules. He then presents the juristic tradition as the disciplined elaboration of those sources and regards its accumulated doctrines as suitable material for contemporary Islamic legislation.

The difficulty is not that revelation plays no role in Islamic criminal law. It plainly does. The difficulty lies in treating revelation, prophetic practice, juristic interpretation, school doctrine, customary judgment, political administration, and modern codification as though they were one undifferentiated body of divine law. They are related, but they are not identical. The central purpose of this chapter is therefore to distinguish the layers of authority that Bahnasi's project brings together. That distinction does not diminish the importance of the Qur'an or the Sunnah. It clarifies where divine communication ends and where human legal construction begins.[22]

21Aḥmad Fatḥī Bahnasi, Al-Ḥudūd fī al-Islām (Alexandria: Muʾassasat Shabāb al-Jāmiʿa, n.d.), 3–5. Bahnasi's introduction presents Islamic jurisprudence as an alternative to imported legislation and as suitable for renewed contemporary codification.

22This distinction also develops an argument already present in Mark A. Gabriel, "Reforming Hudud Ordinances to Reconcile Islamic Criminal Law with International Human Rights Law" (PhD diss., University of Cape Town, 2016), 19–20, where Shariah is distinguished from the human juristic rulings developed through fiqh.

The Qur'anic meaning of ḥudūd. The Arabic word ḥudūd is the plural of ḥadd, meaning a boundary, limit, separating line, or restraint. In the Qur'an, the expression ḥudūd Allāh does not function primarily as the technical name of a closed list of corporal punishments. It refers more broadly to limits established by God that believers should not transgress.[23] These limits appear in contexts involving marriage, divorce, fasting, inheritance, family relations, and other areas of religious and social obligation. The Qur'anic expression therefore has a wider moral and legal meaning than the later technical category of ḥudūd offenses. This distinction is important. To say that God has established limits does not yet tell us that the later juristic category called ḥudūd—with its precise list of offenses, procedural rules, classifications of rights, and consequences of pardon—was delivered as one complete penal system in the Qur'an. The technical category is a product of legal organization.

Jurists gathered different texts, reports, practices, and principles and placed certain offenses within a common classification. They then distinguished those offenses from qiṣāṣ, diyya, and taʿzīr. Bahnasi himself presents this tripartite structure: ḥudūd, retaliation and blood money, and discretionary punishment. He identifies five principal ḥudūd— theft, zinā, false accusation, drinking, and intoxication—and notes that some jurists add rebellion and apostasy.[24] The variation in the list is already significant. If the technical category were simply a self-contained revealed code, one would expect agreement over which offenses belong within it. Yet Bahnasi acknowledges that some jurists include rebellion and apostasy while others do not classify them in the same way. This means that the boundary of the category is itself juristic. Revelation does not arrive as a modern criminal code. A modern criminal code ordinarily identifies the offense, its material elements, the required mental state, available defenses, rules of participation,

---

23See, among other occurrences, Qur'an 2:187, 2:229–30, 4:13–14, 58:4, and 65:1. In these passages the expression ḥudūd Allāh refers broadly to divinely established limits in fasting, marriage, divorce, family relations, and expiation rather than to a closed technical list of corporal punishments.

24Bahnasi, Al-Ḥudūd fī al-Islām, 31–39. Bahnasi distinguishes ḥudūd from qiṣāṣ, diyya, and taʿzīr and records disagreement over the inclusion of rebellion and apostasy within the technical category.

jurisdiction, evidentiary requirements, the sentence, and the authority responsible for enforcement. The Qur'an does not present the ḥudūd in this codified form.[25]

It contains moral commands, prohibitions, narratives, legal principles, and certain stated punishments. The Sunnah supplies additional reports, explanations, judgments, and practices. Jurists then organize those materials into a legal structure. That work requires interpretation. For theft, the Qur'anic text does not independently settle the minimum value, the meaning of protected custody, whether the property must belong entirely to another person, the effect of common ownership, the treatment of family access, necessity, famine, debt, public property, the character of the object taken, or the precise anatomical procedure of amputation. For zinā, the revealed sources do not operate as a complete criminal code without juristic determination of the definition of intercourse, the conditions of iḥṣān, the effect of prior marriage, the number of confessions, the legal effect of retraction, pregnancy as evidence, the relationship between flogging and stoning, and the application of the reported stoning punishment.

For drinking, the Qur'an prohibits intoxicants but does not state a fixed number of lashes.[26] The later punishment emerges from reported practice, analogy, caliphal policy, and juristic disagreement. For apostasy, the Qur'an discusses belief, disbelief, return to disbelief, and divine judgment, but the worldly death penalty is constructed principally through hadith interpretation and the historical association of religious departure with communal and political betrayal. The existence of revelation is therefore not the same as the existence of a complete revealed code.

25For a broad account of the historical formation of Islamic jurisprudence and the difference between juristic discourse and modern state codification, see Wael B. Hallaq, Shariʿa: Theory, Practice, Transformations (Cambridge: Cambridge University Press, 2009).

26Bahnasi, Al-Ḥudūd fī al-Islām, 145–59. His account records the Qur'anic prohibition, varying early methods of beating, and the later disagreement over forty and eighty lashes.

Bahnasi's Definition of the Ḥadd Contains a Juristic Conclusion

Bahnasi defines a ḥadd in the legal sense as a punishment whose amount has been determined, whose enforcement is obligatory, and which is understood as belonging to the right of God.[27] The word "determined" distinguishes the ḥadd from taʿzīr, where the judge may select among different penalties. The phrase "right of God" distinguishes it from retaliation, which belongs substantially to the injured person or the victim's heirs and may therefore be affected by pardon or compensation. This definition appears descriptive, but it contains several major conclusions: that the punishment has been fixed, that it is obligatory, that it belongs principally to God, that private pardon cannot ordinarily extinguish it, and that public authority must enforce it once proven. None of those conclusions follows from the word ḥadd alone. They result from juristic classification. The jurists did not merely discover that a punishment was called a ḥadd. They developed the legal consequences attached to that category. The classification therefore performs substantive legal work. Once the offense is placed among the rights of God, the rules governing pardon, settlement, enforcement, and judicial discretion change. The label does not simply describe the rule. It helps create its operative authority. The "right of God" is a legal category, not a transfer of divine knowledge.

Bahnasi explains that Islamic law recognizes two broad kinds of rights: the right of God and the right of the individual. A right of God concerns a benefit not restricted to one person and is attributed to God because of its general importance. Rights of individuals concern particular interests, such as property and compensation. Some rules combine the two, with either the divine or individual aspect predominating. This classification is central to the classical legal system. It is also frequently misunderstood. A "right of God" does not mean that God personally suffers injury in the way that a human victim suffers injury. Nor does it mean that every procedural and substantive detail was stated directly by God. Rather, the category expresses the juristic judgment that the protected interest is public, religious, or

---

27Bahnasi, Al-Ḥudūd fī al-Islām, 31–39. The definition joins three conclusions: fixed measure, obligatory enforcement, and classification as a right of God.

communal and therefore should not be controlled exclusively by a private claimant. The distinction may have served important purposes. It prevented certain serious matters from being reduced to private bargaining. It expressed the idea that some conduct threatens the wider moral order. It could also restrain powerful individuals from purchasing immunity through compensation. But the category remains a human legal formulation. Jurists determined which interests belong to God, which belong to individuals, which combine both, which aspect predominates, and what procedural consequences follow.

Bahnasi notes, for example, that false accusation combines a public or divine interest with protection of the accused person's reputation.[28] Jurists disagreed over which interest predominates and therefore disagreed over whether the victim's demand is required and whether pardon has legal effect. The disagreement proves that "the right of God" is not a self-applying fact. It must be interpreted.

Classification determines power. The practical effect of these classifications is enormous. If an offense is treated as a private right, the victim may have authority to pardon, settle, or accept compensation. If it is treated as a right of God, the ruler or judge may be required to proceed even where the victim prefers mercy. If it combines both, jurists must determine which interest predominates. The same conduct may therefore produce different legal consequences depending upon its classification. This reveals the central institutional problem: The jurist's act of classification becomes the foundation of the state's coercive authority. When a modern legislature adopts one of these classifications, it is not simply reading a punishment from revelation. It is choosing a theory of legal interests and attaching to it the force of the modern state. That choice determines who may forgive, who may prosecute, who may withdraw, and whether the punishment may be altered.

28Ibid., 35–39. Bahnasi explains the distinction between the rights of God, the rights of individuals, and mixed rights, including disagreement over which element predominates in qadhf.

Divine Prohibition and Fixed Punishment Are Different Questions

One of the most important distinctions in this entire study is the distinction between a religious prohibition and a fixed state punishment. An act may be prohibited without carrying a specified worldly penalty. It may be sinful but left to divine judgment. It may be subject to moral correction, communal discipline, civil consequence, or discretionary punishment. It may be prohibited in one context and regulated differently in another. Bahnasi's presentation occasionally moves too quickly from prohibition to penal enforcement. The alcohol discussion illustrates this clearly. The Qur'anic prohibition of intoxicants is not identical to a fixed numerical punishment. The number of lashes emerged through reports and early governmental practice. Bahnasi himself records that the punishment varied and was not settled in one form during the prophetic period.[29] A similar distinction applies to apostasy. Religious condemnation does not automatically establish a worldly death penalty for the peaceful change of belief. The state must therefore answer two separate questions: Is the conduct religiously prohibited? Should the conduct be criminally punished by the state, and if so, how? The first question belongs to moral and theological interpretation. The second requires a theory of political authority, public harm, proportionality, evidence, and constitutional legitimacy. A religious answer to the first does not eliminate the need to justify the second.

The Sunnah requires interpretation before codification. Bahnasi rightly gives the Sunnah a central place in Islamic law. But the Sunnah does not reach the modern state without interpretation. A reported prophetic judgment raises questions such as: Is the report authentic? Is it general or connected to a particular event? Does it describe a legal obligation or a discretionary response? Was the conduct accompanied by another offense? Was the judgment political, military, pastoral, or strictly judicial? Did later reports qualify or contradict it? Does the report state a minimum, maximum, or example? Does it apply to all places and times? The juristic tradition developed methods for

---

29Ibid., 145–59. The reported practice ranges from striking with hands, garments, sandals, and palm branches to later numerical formulations of forty or eighty lashes.

answering these questions, but those methods did not always produce agreement. The punishment for drinking again provides a clear example. Some reports describe beating with hands, garments, sandals, or palm branches. Later authorities used forty or eighty lashes. Jurists then disagreed over whether the punishment was a fixed ḥadd or partly discretionary. The Sunnah supplies the materials of legal reasoning. It does not remove the need for legal reasoning.

Consensus claims must be examined carefully. Classical jurists frequently invoked ijmāʿ, or consensus, to establish the authority of legal rules. Consensus may function as a source of stability, preventing each generation from reopening every settled question. But its use in criminal law requires special caution. A claim of consensus may refer to universal agreement, agreement among a particular group of jurists, absence of a recorded opponent, dominance of one position, or later acceptance of a rule despite earlier variation. These are not identical. Bahnasi's book repeatedly records disagreement even in matters presented as established ḥudūd. The list of offenses differs. The punishment for drinking differs. The status of rebellion and apostasy differs. Jurists disagree over witnesses, confessions, exemptions, repentance, and the role of the victim. The existence of these disagreements does not make the entire tradition incoherent. It does, however, require caution when one selected position is described as the uncontested command of God.

Analogy reveals human construction. Analogy, or qiyās, plays a major role in the expansion and organization of Islamic law. The reasoning attributed to ʿAlī regarding the drinking punishment is illustrative.[30] Intoxication may lead to irrational speech; irrational speech may lead to false accusation; false accusation carries eighty lashes; therefore eighty lashes may be imposed for drinking. That is legal reasoning. It is not a direct numerical command found in the Qur'an. Analogy may be sophisticated and principled. It may also be debated, rejected, or limited. The Iraqi and Hijazi disagreement over the meaning of khamr demonstrates this. Some jurists extend the ruling and the name to every intoxicant. Others accept the prohibition of other

30Ibid., 154–59. The argument attributed to ʿAlī links intoxication to irrational speech, irrational speech to false accusation, and qadhf to eighty lashes, thereby illustrating analogical and policy-based construction rather than a Qur'anic numerical command.

intoxicants but resist extending the linguistic name khamr through analogy. The disagreement shows that even where the moral conclusion is similar, the legal route differs. Once analogy contributes to the definition or punishment of an offense, the final doctrine cannot accurately be described as revelation alone.

Custom and Social Conditions Enter the Supposedly Fixed Law

Custom appears repeatedly in the law of theft. The meaning of protected custody depends partly upon how people ordinarily preserve particular kinds of property.[31] What counts as secure storage differs according to place, time, object, occupation, and social practice. The legal definition therefore changes as society changes. The same is true of value. The minimum threshold depends upon monetary measures, market conditions, and juristic calculation. The treatment of different types of property also reflects historical economic assumptions. Bahnasi recognizes the adaptability of Islamic jurisprudence and praises its ability to respond to changing conditions. But this adaptability creates a tension. If the offense depends upon changing custom, value, economic structure, and social access, then the state is not enforcing a timeless rule without modification. It is reconstructing the offense in every new legal environment. The punishment may remain physically fixed while the conditions activating it change through human judgment.

Political practice becomes doctrine. The development of Islamic criminal law was also shaped by rulers, caliphs, governors, and judges. ʿUmar's suspension of amputation during famine is frequently cited as evidence of mercy and contextual judgment. It is indeed evidence of contextual judgment. But it also demonstrates that political authority interpreted the conditions under which the punishment could justly operate. Similarly, the increase of the drinking punishment reflects consultation and policy. The treatment of rebels developed within actual civil conflicts. The doctrine of apostasy was shaped by the wars that followed the Prophet's death and by the close connection between

---

31Ibid., 70–89. Bahnasi's discussion of ḥirz makes protected custody dependent in part upon custom, the character of the property, location, occupation, and ordinary methods of preservation.

religious allegiance, political membership, taxation, and military loyalty. Historical practice therefore entered the juristic tradition. Once that happens, the modern state must distinguish among revelation, prophetic example, emergency governance, caliphal policy, civil-war doctrine, and later juristic generalization. Without that distinction, contingent political decisions may be transformed into universal divine commands.

Codification creates a new law even when it claims restoration. Classical Islamic law developed through a plurality of jurists, schools, judges, and local practices. A modern criminal code operates differently. The modern state must write one enforceable rule. It must decide which school to follow, how to define the offense, which defenses to recognize, which witnesses are competent, whether confession may be withdrawn, which punishment applies, whether the victim may pardon, and which court possesses jurisdiction. Bahnasi welcomes selection among the schools and argues that modern Islamic legislation should not be limited to one inherited school.[32] This allows flexibility. But it also reveals the creative role of the legislature. A code assembled from selected Mālikī, Ḥanafī, Shāfiʿī, Ḥanbalī, Ẓāhirī, Shiʿi, and individual opinions did not exist as such in the classical period. It is a new legal product. Its provisions may be inspired by Islamic jurisprudence, but the act of selection, combination, exclusion, and formulation belongs to the modern state. The state cannot honestly claim that it is merely copying one complete divine code. It is legislating.

The problem of selective divine authority. The modern legislature may select one opinion because it appears more practical, stricter, more lenient, or better suited to current conditions. But once selected, the rule may be presented publicly as "God's law." This creates an asymmetry. The state exercises human choice when drafting the rule but invokes divine authority when enforcing it. The choice remains political, while the criticism is treated as theological. This is one of the most dangerous features of restorationist codification. The government may claim divine authority for a humanly selected definition, divine immutability for a historically contested rule, and may portray citizens who challenge

---

32Ibid., 3–5. Bahnasi explicitly resists confining modern Islamic legislation to one school and treats juristic plurality as a resource from which contemporary lawmakers may select.

the legislation as religiously disobedient. The result is not simply religious law. It is political authority protected by sacred language.

The Difference Between Fidelity and Literal Transfer

Rejecting the direct transfer of the classical penal system into modern legislation does not require rejecting revelation. A society may remain faithful to the moral purposes of revelation while adopting different legal instruments. The Qur'anic concern for property may be preserved through restitution and proportionate criminal law. The concern for reputation may be protected through defamation remedies. The concern for sobriety may be addressed through public-health law and punishment of harmful conduct. The concern for family responsibility may remain within moral, religious, and civil law. The concern for public safety may be protected through modern laws against violence and armed criminality. Fidelity does not require identical institutional form across every century. The question is whether the moral purpose is preserved, not whether every historical penal mechanism is reproduced.

Juristic disagreement is not a defect—but it defeats claims of automatic enforcement. The argument of this chapter should not be misunderstood as hostility toward juristic disagreement. Disagreement is evidence of intellectual seriousness. It shows that jurists confronted difficult texts and changing circumstances. It may reveal humility and recognition of uncertainty. The problem arises only when a disputed juristic conclusion is transferred into irreversible state punishment and then described as though no human judgment remains. The existence of disagreement requires the state to admit that it has chosen, that another interpretation was possible, that its judgment may be wrong, and that it bears responsibility for the consequences. That responsibility becomes overwhelming where the punishment cannot be reversed.

The central distinction. The legal structure examined in Bahnasi's book contains at least six distinct layers: Qur'anic revelation, including moral limits, prohibitions, and certain punishments. Prophetic practice and reported Sunnah, which require authentication and interpretation. Juristic classification, including the technical category of ḥudūd and the distinction between divine and private rights. School doctrine, in which definitions, conditions, and punishments were organized differently. Political and judicial practice, including caliphal policy, emergency measures, and historical enforcement. Modern codification, in which the contemporary state selects and combines particular doctrines. These layers may form a connected tradition, but they do not possess the same authority. To treat all six as direct revelation is to conceal the human role in the creation of operative law.

Conclusion

Bahnasi's restorationist project depends upon the movement from divine revelation to positive state law. Yet that movement passes through multiple stages of human interpretation. The Qur'an establishes moral and legal limits but does not present one complete modern penal code. The Sunnah provides essential guidance but requires interpretation. Jurists developed the technical category of ḥudūd, classified rights as belonging to God or individuals, defined the offenses, resolved evidentiary questions, and attached legal consequences to each classification. Schools disagreed. Rulers exercised policy. Custom shaped application. Modern legislatures must then choose among those inherited positions. The resulting law may be Islamic in inspiration and historical origin. It is not free from human authorship. The decisive principle is therefore: The authority of revelation must not be used to conceal the responsibility of interpretation. A modern government that chooses one disputed juristic position and enforces it through police, courts, corporal punishment, or execution is exercising human political power. It must justify that power through justice, proportionality, equality, evidence, and constitutional accountability. It cannot avoid responsibility merely by naming its choice the right of God. This conclusion leads directly to the next chapter:

Chapter Three

The "Right of God" and the Sacralization of Punishment

Among the most consequential concepts in classical Islamic criminal jurisprudence is the distinction between the right of God and the right of the individual. The distinction is not merely theoretical. It affects who may initiate proceedings, whether settlement or pardon is possible, how far the ruler or judge may exercise discretion, and whether punishment must continue once the offense has been legally established. Aḥmad Fatḥī Bahnasi places the ḥudūd principally within the category of the rights of God. He explains that a right of God concerns an interest whose benefit is not confined to one person, whereas a right of the individual protects a particular human interest such as property, bodily security, reputation, or compensation. Some offenses contain both elements, but the jurists must determine which predominates.[33]

This classification is foundational to Bahnasi's legal project because it is the point at which punishment becomes sacralized. By sacralization, I do not mean that Bahnasi treats suffering as an object of worship or as an end in itself. I mean that a punishment is placed within a legal category attributed to God and thereby acquires a special immunity from ordinary alteration, pardon, or abolition. Once the offense is classified as a right of God, political authority no longer appears to be selecting a penal policy. It presents itself as executing a divine obligation. The movement from juristic classification to apparent divine necessity is the central concern of this chapter.

The Legal Meaning of the "Right of God"

In Bahnasi's presentation, a right of God is associated with a general or communal benefit rather than an interest belonging exclusively to one claimant. The attribution emphasizes the seriousness and public character of the rule and removes it from complete private control. The

33Aḥmad Fatḥī Bahnasi, Al-Ḥudūd fī al-Islām (Alexandria: Muʾassasat Shabāb al-Jāmiʿa, n.d.), 30–39. Bahnasi distinguishes ḥudūd from qiṣāṣ, diyya, and taʿzīr and explains the division between the rights of God and the rights of individuals.

individual cannot ordinarily waive the right because it does not belong solely to him or her. The classification therefore has concrete consequences: private settlement may not terminate the case, pardon may be restricted, the injured person may lose authority over the proceedings, and the ruler or judge may become responsible for enforcement.[34]

The concept served an intelligible purpose within the classical system. It prevented certain offenses from being reduced to private transactions and could protect the community where a victim was intimidated, bribed, or unwilling to proceed. A wealthy offender could not always purchase immunity merely because an individual claimant accepted payment. Yet the same classification can also remove punishment from ordinary human judgment. The issue is not whether law may protect a public interest; every developed legal system does so. The issue is whether describing an interest as the right of God establishes that one inherited punishment is permanently immune from moral, legislative, and constitutional review.

Public interest and divine ownership are not identical. Theft may threaten security of property; ḥirāba may threaten travelers and public order; false accusation may injure both an individual and the moral life of the community; intoxication may threaten reason and safety; and unlawful sexual conduct may be understood as affecting family responsibility and lineage. These are social claims capable of legal and moral debate. But the conclusion that conduct affects society does not prove that one particular punishment belongs permanently to God. Modern criminal law also protects public interests and may prosecute murder, domestic violence, corruption, trafficking, or organized crime even where an individual victim wishes to remain silent. Those laws nevertheless remain subject to amendment, proportionality, constitutional review, evidentiary safeguards, and public criticism. A public interest can justify public concern without making the chosen punishment sacred.

34Bahnasi, Al-Ḥudūd fī al-Islām, 34–39. His account connects the right of God to a general benefit and explains the consequences for enforcement, pardon, and private control.

The Victim and the Restriction of Pardon

The effect of classification becomes especially visible in Bahnasi's discussion of qadhf, or false accusation of unlawful sexual conduct. The offense plainly protects the reputation of a particular person, yet it is also treated as safeguarding public morality. Jurists therefore disagreed over whether the divine or individual element predominates, whether the victim's complaint is required, whether pardon is effective, and whether enforcement may continue independently of the injured person. The disagreement is important because it demonstrates that the status of the right is not self-evident. It must be constructed through juristic reasoning, and that reasoning determines who controls the case.[35]

A specific human being bears the immediate injury of false accusation. His or her dignity, family relationships, social standing, and emotional well-being may be damaged. The victim may prefer apology, retraction, compensation, reconciliation, privacy, or an end to public proceedings. Yet where the right of God is considered predominant, the legal system may treat those preferences as secondary and insist upon corporal punishment in the name of a wider moral interest. The question is therefore unavoidable: does attributing the punishment to God protect the victim, or does it allow political authority to take possession of the victim's injury? A just system may recognize public harm without erasing the agency of the person most directly affected.

The restriction of pardon reveals an equally difficult contrast. In qiṣāṣ, where a person has been killed or physically injured, the victim or the victim's family may possess a recognized role in forgiveness, compensation, or retaliation. Bahnasi distinguishes this from the ḥudūd, whose punishments are treated as determined and ordinarily unavailable for private waiver after proof has been completed. The moral result can appear inverted: where a human injury is most direct, room for human pardon may remain; where the offense is associated more abstractly with God or public morality, mercy becomes legally narrower. The classification risks making mercy weakest precisely where punishment has been sacralized.[36]

35Bahnasi, Al-Ḥudūd fī al-Islām, 37–39. On qadhf as an offense combining the right of God and the right of the individual, and the juristic disagreement over which element predominates.

Fixed Punishment and Human Decision

Bahnasi contrasts the ḥudūd with taʿzīr. In discretionary punishment, the judge or ruler may consider the seriousness of the conduct, the offender's circumstances, the likelihood of reform, social conditions, deterrence, and the public interest. The punishment may be adjusted because flexibility is openly recognized. The ḥudūd are presented differently. Once the offense is established under the required conditions, the judge is not expected to replace the prescribed penalty merely because another response appears more humane, useful, or proportionate. A flexible theory of punishment therefore becomes rigid once a juristic classification places the conduct within the ḥudūd.[37]

The expression "fixed by the lawgiver" creates the impression that the punishment reaches the judge directly from revelation. But before enforcement can occur, human authorities must decide which offenses belong to the category, what conduct satisfies each definition, which school governs, what threshold applies, what evidence is sufficient, which defenses are recognized, whether repentance has legal effect, whether the victim's demand is required, and whether the divine or private interest predominates. These decisions are not peripheral. They determine whether the punishment exists in the particular case. The final sentence may be described as fixed, but the route to it is constructed through human judgment.

The contradiction can be stated plainly:

> *Human beings decide whether a punishment attributed to God has become mandatory and then deny themselves authority to reconsider it because they have classified it as divine.*

The system begins with interpretation and ends with claimed immutability. That structure matters profoundly when the outcome is

---

36See Bahnasi, Al-Ḥudūd fī al-Islām, 32–39, for the distinction between fixed ḥudūd and qiṣāṣ or diyya, in which the injured person or heirs may possess a role in pardon or compensation.

37Bahnasi, Al-Ḥudūd fī al-Islām, 20–39. Bahnasi presents taʿzīr as discretionary and adaptable while defining the ḥadd as a punishment whose amount is determined and whose enforcement is obligatory.

flogging, amputation, stoning, crucifixion, or execution. The more irreversible the punishment, the less acceptable it is to conceal the human choices that activate it.

Sacralization and the Status of Criticism

An ordinary criminal statute may be challenged as ineffective, discriminatory, disproportionate, outdated, unconstitutional, or unjust. A punishment classified as the right of God is more difficult to examine in those terms. Criticism may be portrayed not merely as disagreement with government but as resistance to divine law. A citizen who questions amputation may be accused of rejecting the Qur'an; a scholar who questions stoning may be accused of denying the Sunnah; a reformer who opposes death for peaceful apostasy may be accused of weakening Islam; and a lawyer who challenges unequal procedure may be accused of preferring foreign law to revelation. Sacralization therefore does more than preserve punishment. It narrows the intellectual and moral space in which punishment may be examined.[38]

The modern authority gains a powerful rhetorical advantage. It presents itself not as the author of punishment but as the obedient executor of God's command. Yet the same authority has selected the school, definition, evidentiary rules, jurisdiction, procedure, and institutional machinery through which the sentence becomes possible. The state, regime, or armed movement claiming to enforce Islamic criminal law is therefore interpreter and executor at the same time. Its declaration of modest obedience may conceal an extensive exercise of political power.

In theory the right belongs to God; in practice enforcement belongs to rulers, judges, prosecutors, police, ministries, prison officials, religious councils, and legislative bodies. The right enters the world through human institutions. This creates the danger that the right of God will become, in practical effect, the right of government. Resistance to

---

38Mark A. Gabriel, "Reforming Hudud Ordinances to Reconcile Islamic Criminal Law with International Human Rights Law" (PhD diss., University of Cape Town, 2016), 17–20. The dissertation identifies the claim that ḥudūd are rights of God as a principal obstacle to reform and distinguishes divine Shariah from fallible juristic construction.

the ruler may be represented as resistance to divine law, criticism of the court as criticism of religion, and demand for reform as hostility toward Islam. The danger becomes clearest in the doctrines of rebellion and apostasy, but it is present throughout the penal system.

Human Fallibility and Procedural Avoidance

Divine attribution does not eliminate human fallibility. Witnesses may lie, confessions may be coerced, judges may misunderstand, legislatures may select the wrong opinion, prosecutors may act selectively, religious institutions may become sectarian, and rulers may use morality law against opponents. None of these possibilities disappears because the sentence is called the right of God. The attribution may make error more dangerous by increasing institutional confidence while reducing accountability. A fallible authority becomes most dangerous when it believes its judgment carries divine certainty.

The classical tradition responded to the danger of severe and irreversible punishment through doctrines of restraint. The ḥudūd were to be averted in cases of doubt; confession could be discouraged; retraction might be accepted; private wrongdoing was not always to be exposed; witnesses were subject to demanding conditions; and judges were urged not to extend liability recklessly. These doctrines reflect genuine moral caution. They also reveal an internal tension. Because the punishment is treated as fixed, mercy frequently appears through defects in proof rather than through open reconsideration of the sentence. The system cannot easily alter the punishment, so it narrows the path to conviction; it cannot ordinarily grant pardon after completion of proof, so it seeks uncertainty before that point.[39]

Mercy thereby becomes indirect. In a flexible legal order it may be expressed openly through mitigation, pardon, suspended sentence, proportionality, rehabilitation, restorative justice, or legislative amendment. Under a rigid ḥadd structure, mercy may depend upon doubt, disputed ownership, incomplete testimony, retracted confession,

---

39The maxim that ḥudūd should be averted in cases of doubt is discussed throughout the classical and modern literature. See Gabriel, "Reforming Hudud Ordinances," 160–97; and Mohammad Hashim Kamali, Shariah Law: An Introduction (Oxford: Oneworld, 2008), 204 –18.

necessity, or another technical failure. The result is paradoxical. The law declares the punishment perfectly just, yet judicial mercy often requires avoiding the point at which it must be imposed. A system confident in the substantive justice of its sentence should not need to depend so heavily upon procedural escape.

Public Welfare and the Circular Argument

Bahnasi connects the ḥudūd to the protection of lineage, property, life, reason, public morality, and social order. These purposes are legitimate subjects of law. But public welfare cannot be presumed merely because an inherited punishment has been classified as serving it. The state must still ask whether the punishment actually prevents the harm, whether it is proportionate, whether a less destructive measure is available, whether enforcement is unequal, whether victims are discouraged from reporting, whether the rule creates secrecy or political abuse, and whether the consequence can be corrected after error. Public interest is not a self-proving phrase. It is a claim requiring evidence and moral justification.[40]

The defense of the ḥudūd can otherwise become circular. The punishment is called a right of God and is therefore said to be fixed; because God fixed it, it is assumed to be necessarily just; because it is necessarily just, human beings may not alter it; and because they may not alter it, its status as the right of God appears confirmed. This reasoning is incomplete unless the divine origin of every operative detail has first been established independently. Bahnasi's own work records substantial disagreement over the offenses, proof, status, repentance, pardon, and enforcement. A modern authority cannot invoke the right of God without identifying which human interpretation it has selected and accepting responsibility for that selection.

A mature theory of justice must distinguish the interests of the victim, the interests of society, and the authority of government. The right-of-God classification can collapse the last two. Because an offense is said to affect society, the government claims authority; because government claims authority, its punishment is presented as serving

---

40Bahnasi, Al-Ḥudūd fī al-Islām, 7–29, on deterrence, public protection, individual correction, and the general purposes of punishment in Islamic law.

God's right. But society and government are not identical. A regime may invoke public morality while protecting its own power, prosecute selectively, ignore politically inconvenient victims, or use sacred language to silence the community it claims to represent. The public character of an offense therefore cannot justify unlimited political authority.

The Constitutional Alternative

A constitutional system can protect public interests without sacralizing punishment. It may prosecute serious offenses despite private pressure, restrict settlement where coercion or continuing danger is present, protect victims, and impose proportionate sanctions through independent courts. Most importantly, it may permit laws to be reviewed, revised, or abolished. This does not require hostility toward religion. Moral and religious values may inform public law, but coercive punishment remains a human institutional act for which human authorities must answer.[41]

The argument is not that law should be morally empty or that Islam should have no place in public ethical discussion. It is narrower and more fundamental: no state, regime, or armed movement claiming to enforce Islamic criminal law should place its coercive acts beyond criticism by attributing its own selected punishment directly to God. A Muslim society may condemn theft, violence, false accusation, intoxication, and betrayal; it may draw guidance from the Qur'an and Sunnah and preserve repentance, accountability, family responsibility, and public protection. But amputation, flogging, and execution are performed by human officials. They cannot be removed from moral scrutiny by sacred attribution.

41For the modern transformation of plural juristic doctrine into centralized state law, see Wael B. Hallaq, Shari'a: Theory, Practice, Transformations (Cambridge: Cambridge University Press, 2009), 357–443; and Noah Feldman, The Fall and Rise of the Islamic State (Princeton, NJ: Princeton University Press, 2008), 6–15, 100–121.

Conclusion

The classification of the ḥudūd as rights of God is one of the most powerful legal ideas in Bahnasi's book. It helps explain why punishment is treated as fixed, why pardon may be restricted, why settlement may be unavailable, and why public authority is expected to enforce the sentence after proof has been completed. Yet the category does more than organize doctrine. It transforms a juristic classification into an apparent divine mandate, reduces the visible responsibility of the legislature, narrows the authority of victims, restricts mercy, and places criticism under theological suspicion.

The conclusion is straightforward:

> *A public interest may justify state concern, but it does not justify placing one humanly interpreted punishment beyond human accountability.*

The right of God cannot become a shield behind which a state, regime, or armed movement conceals its own choices. Once an authority selects, codifies, prosecutes, and enforces a punishment, it bears full responsibility for what it does. Its law must remain answerable to justice, equality, proportionality, evidence, and human dignity. Yet sacralization does not operate only inside legal doctrine or state institutions. Before turning to the individual offenses, the next chapter examines how the claim of divine immutability enters the public religious mind and can make the very act of questioning appear spiritually dangerous.

Chapter Four

The Book on the Bedroom Shelf: Ḥudūd Orthodoxy and the Policing of Muslim Thought

Many years ago, while I was still living in Egypt, I read a small Arabic book entitled Wujūb Taṭbīq al-Ḥudūd al-Sharʿiyya—The Obligation to Implement the Sharīʿa Ḥudūd—by ʿAbd al-Raḥmān ʿAbd al-Khāliq. I knew the argument well. The book was not a major work of Islamic jurisprudence, nor did I regard it as representing the highest level of scholarly reasoning found in the classical legal tradition. It belonged to another category of Islamic literature: direct, confident, easily circulated, religiously forceful, and written for a public much larger than the circle of specialist jurists.[42]

Years later, however, I encountered the same book again under circumstances that changed the way I understood the influence of such literature.

I was visiting a Muslim family in Europe. The family had welcomed me into their home, and we spent much of the day together. The mother prepared an extraordinary meal and continued throughout the visit to extend the kind of hospitality familiar to anyone raised in the Arab world. Her daughter helped her. The father was an ordinary hardworking man who had spent much of his adult life building a home and raising his children after immigrating to Europe. Nothing about him gave me reason to regard him as a dangerous man. He was respectful. He was a father concerned about his family. He was also struggling deeply with a religious disagreement involving his only son.

At one point during an increasingly serious conversation, the father went into his bedroom and returned carrying a book. I recognized it immediately. It was Wujūb Taṭbīq al-Ḥudūd al-Sharʿiyya. I had read it years before in Egypt. Now I was looking at another copy of the same book in the hands of a Muslim father in Europe.

42ʿAbd al-Raḥmān ʿAbd al-Khāliq, Wujūb Taṭbīq al-Ḥudūd al-Sharʿiyya, 2nd ed. (Kuwait: Maktabat Ibn Taymiyyah, 1984). The second-edition preface is dated 1404 AH/1983, while the publication page gives 1404 AH/1984 for the edition.

He held the book as an authority for what he believed God required, and in the intensity of the discussion he expressed the conviction that two people sitting peacefully in his home deserved death because of the religious choices they had made. His daughter reacted immediately. She protested against what her father was saying. This was her brother. She loved him. And I was a guest in their home. Her mother was quieter, but her discomfort was evident. She continued preparing and serving food, maintaining the dignity and hospitality of the household while a painful conflict unfolded around her.

I was surprised to see the book. I was not surprised by the father's reasoning. I understood where it came from.

That distinction is important. It would be easy to tell this story as evidence of an angry or intolerant Muslim father. That would miss almost everything that mattered about what I witnessed. I did not see a monster sitting across from me. I saw a father caught between two enormously powerful forces: his love for his son and what he understood to be his obligation before God.

His son was his only son. In many traditional Middle Eastern families, an only son can carry a particular emotional weight. A father may see in him continuity of name, memory, and family life extending into another generation. The father's distress therefore could not be reduced to theological disagreement. He loved his son. That was precisely what made the situation painful.

This encounter is illustrative, not a sociological sample. One family cannot establish the prevalence of an attitude across Muslim communities. Its value here is narrower: it shows how a doctrinal claim, already present in a widely circulated religious text, can move from the page into the moral life of an ordinary household. The broader argument of this chapter therefore rests on the text and its reasoning, while the family encounter shows what that reasoning can look like when it becomes personal.

When Love and Obedience Appear to Collide

A Muslim who has spent a lifetime hearing the Qur'ān knows the language of religious loyalty intimately. Qur'ān 9:24 presents one of its most demanding formulations: if fathers, sons, brothers, spouses, relatives, wealth, commerce, and homes become dearer than God, His

Messenger, and striving in His way, the believer is warned to wait for God's command.[43]

The verse does not prescribe a punishment for apostasy. It should not be made to say something it does not say. Its significance here is different. It establishes a hierarchy of loyalty. Fathers, sons, spouses, family, property, livelihood, and home—all the things around which ordinary human life is constructed—must remain subordinate to loyalty to God.

For the believer, this can be spiritually meaningful. But when such a hierarchy is joined to a legal interpretation according to which particular acts of religious dissent constitute offenses against God, and when questioning those rulings is itself portrayed as rebellion against divine authority, an extraordinary burden can be placed upon the human conscience. A father may then find himself asking not simply whether he loves his son, but whether loving his son in a particular way means placing his son above God.

This is where books such as Wujūb Taṭbīq al-Ḥudūd al-Sharʿiyya acquire an importance far greater than their scholarly sophistication would suggest.

The book begins from an uncompromising premise. Islamic Sharīʿa is presented as a complete divine order regulating worship, family, inheritance, commerce, politics, morality, and criminal punishment. The author contrasts this order with human legislation, which he repeatedly associates with corruption, injustice, moral decay, and departure from God's guidance. He explicitly links the application of Sharīʿa with blessing, prosperity, justice, security, and social well-being. In his argument, establishing the ḥudūd does not merely punish crime; it participates in restoring an entire divinely ordered society.[44]

The implication is powerful because the reader is not being asked to compare two competing criminal-justice models. He is being asked to choose between the law of God and the law of human beings. That is an entirely different psychological proposition.

43Qur'ān 9:24. The verse establishes a hierarchy of loyalty; it does not itself prescribe a worldly punishment for apostasy.

44ʿAbd al-Khāliq, Wujūb Taṭbīq al-Ḥudūd al-Sharʿiyya, 9–13. These pages connect comprehensive Sharīʿa observance, including the ḥudūd, with blessing, prosperity, justice, social order, and protection from corruption.

The author proceeds to warn of the consequences of abandoning divine law, employing Qur'ānic accounts of earlier religious communities and presenting their failure to uphold God's commands as a warning to Muslims. He portrays social and political decline as a consequence of departing from divine legislation and argues that the Muslim community cannot expect strength or divine favor while abandoning the Sharīʿa.[45]

Then the argument becomes still more serious. A chapter bears the unequivocal heading, Radd al-ḥukm al-sharʿī kufr—Rejecting the Sharīʿa ruling is unbelief.

The author explains that acknowledgment of God's legislation is part of faith and submission. He then identifies such punishments as theft, killing, adultery, drinking, highway robbery, and other offenses as well-known Sharīʿa rulings. Most importantly, he argues that where a ruling is certainly established in religion, denying it or rejecting it can constitute unbelief that removes a person from Islam. He specifically rejects objections based upon claims that such legislation does not suit contemporary people or modern times, or that it is barbaric or objectionable. Near the end of the book, after defending stoning, the author returns to the same boundary: he treats belief in the punishment's obligatory status as a matter of creed and declares its denial unbelief.[46]

At this point the legal discussion has changed fundamentally. The reader is no longer merely being told, "This is the correct jurisprudential position." He is being told, in effect, "Your religious identity may depend upon accepting it." That distinction goes to the heart of the problem.

The Power of the Non-Specialist Religious Voice

During my years of studying Islamic history and culture and living within the Muslim intellectual world, I learned that the scholars who

---

45Ibid., 13–22. The section "al-Taḥdhīr min Tark Iqāmat al-Ḥudūd" warns that abandoning divine legislation brings loss and punishment and uses earlier religious communities as cautionary examples.

46Ibid., 23–24, 63–64. The chapter heading on p. 23 states "Radd al-ḥukm al-sharʿī kufr" ("Rejecting the Sharīʿa ruling is unbelief"). In the concluding defense of stoning, the author likewise states that belief in its obligatory status is a matter of creed and that denying it is unbelief.

write the most sophisticated books are not necessarily the people who exercise the greatest influence over the public mind. Academic jurists may debate evidence, conditions, exceptions, legal capacity, evidentiary standards, competing schools of interpretation, and the circumstances under which a rule may or may not be enforced. Their discussions may fill hundreds of pages. In my experience, many ordinary Muslims encounter the conclusions of such debates indirectly rather than by reading the specialist works themselves.

In my experience, a short religious booklet can have far greater influence. It can be sold inexpensively. It can be carried from one country to another. I have seen arguments of this kind move from the printed page into sermons, religious lessons, recordings, broadcasts, and conversations within families. Its language is simple enough to repeat: God commanded this. The Muslim must submit. Human law is inferior. Abandoning divine legislation brings corruption. Rejecting an established ruling may be unbelief.[47]

There is little room in such language for uncertainty. Indeed, uncertainty itself begins to appear spiritually suspicious.

This helps explain one of the most significant obstacles confronting serious reform of Islamic criminal law. The obstacle is not located only within books of classical fiqh, nor only within ministries of justice or religious institutions. It exists in the public religious imagination.

An ordinary Muslim may privately struggle with amputation, flogging, stoning, or capital punishment. He may wonder whether these penalties can be reconciled with justice in his own time. He may be troubled by cases of political manipulation, unreliable courts, coerced confessions, discriminatory enforcement, poverty, or authoritarian government. He may even experience an immediate moral hesitation when confronted with the suffering of another human being. But before he can investigate those concerns, another question may enter his mind: Am I questioning God? That question can end the inquiry before it begins.

47The author's own first-edition preface frames the booklet as an intervention in public religious debate. He complains that major media and educational platforms had fallen into the hands of people who ignored or opposed Sharīʿa and explains that his newspaper articles were written to confront that situation. Ibid., 5–7.

How Silence Becomes Consensus

This produces a phenomenon rarely addressed adequately in discussions of Islamic criminal law. Silence can be mistaken for agreement.

Suppose a Muslim doubts privately whether a particular ḥadd should be enforced. He has heard throughout his life that the punishment comes directly from God. He has heard that opposing God's law may amount to disbelief. Perhaps he has watched religious figures publicly denounce people who question established rulings. He knows what could happen socially if he voices his doubts. So he remains silent. Others may do the same for similar reasons. When that pattern repeats, public silence can begin to resemble public agreement.

Their silence is then observed and described as evidence that the Muslim community accepts the doctrine unanimously. The next person who raises the question is therefore told: "No Muslim has a problem with this. Only enemies of Islam oppose it." Fear has helped create silence, and silence is then used to manufacture the appearance of complete agreement. The cycle reinforces itself.

This does not mean that classical Islamic jurisprudence contains no consensus or that every established legal principle is merely the result of intimidation. Such a claim would be historically careless. The point is different. Public religious consensus and technical juristic consensus are not the same thing. The apparent unanimity of ordinary Muslims cannot automatically be treated as evidence that each individual has freely examined the underlying legal questions and reached an independent conclusion. Some may never have believed that they were permitted to ask the question.

This is what I mean by the policing of the Muslim public mind. The policing does not always require a government, a religious police force, or a criminal court. Sometimes it operates through a sentence spoken from a pulpit. Sometimes through a television preacher. Sometimes through a small book placed on a shelf in a bedroom.

A Complete System—or No Reform at All

There is another revealing element in ʿAbd al-Khāliq's argument. He does not merely defend particular punishments. He objects to treating them as isolated legal provisions that can be inserted into otherwise modern legal systems. His larger argument is that Islam constitutes a single integrated order and cannot properly be divided according to human preference.

In his discussion of imprisonment, for example, he argues that prison is not, in itself, the prescribed Sharīʿa punishment that modern legal systems have made it. He distinguishes limited detention from the modern institution of imprisonment and portrays contemporary prisons as schools of criminality, sources of moral corruption, economic burdens upon the state, and instruments through which rulers can oppress people. Not all of his criticism of prisons should simply be dismissed. Prisons can indeed degrade human beings. They can harden offenders, separate families, impose enormous financial burdens, and become instruments of state abuse. A serious reformer should be willing to acknowledge that.[48]

But the author's conclusion is not therefore that Muslim societies should rethink punishment altogether. His conclusion is that they should return to the divinely prescribed penal order. He also argues against using Sharīʿa rulings to legitimize or patch man-made legal systems. The logic is again comprehensive: Islam must be taken as one whole, rather than selectively combined with legislation produced outside the divine system.

This position has profound consequences for reform. If Islam is defined as one indivisible legal system, and if challenging one certainly established ruling becomes a challenge to divine sovereignty, then the reformer can easily find himself accused not of proposing a different jurisprudential reading, but of dismantling Islam piece by piece. The argument protects itself.

The Difference Between Revelation and Interpretation

Here we reach the distinction upon which much of this book rests. God is divine. The Qurʾān is revelation within Islamic faith. But human interpretation of revelation remains human.[49]

48Ibid., 28–40. ʿAbd al-Khāliq argues that imprisonment is not itself a prescribed Sharīʿa punishment in the modern sense and criticizes prisons as schools of criminality, sources of sexual and moral corruption, economic burdens, and instruments of oppression.

49For the distinction between divine Sharīʿa and fallible juristic law, see Mark A. Gabriel, "Reforming Hudud Ordinances to Reconcile

This distinction should be elementary, yet in discussions of the ḥudūd it is repeatedly blurred. A jurist reads a text, evaluates a report, determines its authenticity, reconciles it with another text, develops rules of evidence, defines an offense, determines the requisite intention, establishes defenses, distinguishes one category of punishment from another, decides the role of political authority, and constructs a legal doctrine. Every step involves human reason.

To acknowledge this does not insult Islamic jurisprudence. It explains how Islamic jurisprudence came into existence. The extraordinary richness of the classical schools themselves bears witness to this fact. Jurists disagreed because interpretation was taking place. They disagreed over evidence, analogy, public interest, custom, necessity, doubt, procedure, and the boundaries of judicial discretion. If every conclusion had simply descended from heaven in finished legal form, such an enormous jurisprudential tradition would scarcely have been necessary.

The danger begins when a human interpretation succeeds in clothing itself entirely in divine authority. Then questioning the interpretation becomes questioning God. And when that occurs, reform becomes psychologically terrifying long before it becomes legally difficult.

The Father and the Book

This is why I return to the father I met in Europe. I do not know everything that passed through his mind that evening. I would not presume to reconstruct thoughts he never expressed. But I understood enough of the world from which his reasoning came to recognize the conflict.

He had before him his son, whom he loved. He also had before him a religious framework that had taught him that obedience to God must supersede every human attachment. When the discussion became difficult, he went to his bedroom and brought back a book.

I have thought about that gesture many times. Perhaps he was reaching for certainty. The human situation before him was

---

Islamic Criminal Law with International Human Rights Law" (PhD diss., University of Cape Town, 2016), 19–20; Mohammad Hashim Kamali, Shariʿah Law: An Introduction (Oxford: Oneworld, 2008), 14–28.

complicated. His emotions were complicated. His family relationships were complicated. The book was not complicated. The book told him where divine authority stood.

That is one reason such literature can become more influential than scholarly jurisprudence. Complexity can be intellectually honest, but certainty is emotionally powerful. A jurist may say that a legal question requires distinctions. An ideological writer can say that God has already decided. For the frightened believer, the second voice can be far more compelling.

This is also why I cannot portray that father simply as a cruel man. To do so would allow us to avoid the real problem. If he were merely evil, the solution would be easy: condemn the man and move on. But he was not simply evil. He was a hardworking father who had raised a family, welcomed a guest into his home, and remained capable of ordinary human kindness. His wife showed remarkable dignity. His daughter loved her brother enough to confront her father. The household itself was filled with signs of human attachment. And yet a doctrinal interpretation was powerful enough to enter that home and place those attachments under judgment.

The Ḥudūd Before the Courtroom

When scholars evaluate the implementation of Islamic criminal law, attention naturally falls upon states that carry out amputations, floggings, executions, or other corporal punishments. Those cases are important. They must be studied. But they reveal only part of the influence of the ḥudūd tradition.

A punishment can exercise power even when it is never formally imposed. A person can be told that he deserves death even though no court will execute him. A woman can live in fear of moral accusation even though no judge has convicted her. A questioning Muslim can silence himself because he fears being called an unbeliever. A son can become estranged from his father because a theological doctrine stands between them. A scholar can avoid examining a difficult question because he knows the social consequences of crossing an established religious boundary.

This is the pre-judicial life of punishment. The ḥadd exists first as an idea. The idea establishes moral boundaries. Those boundaries shape communities. Communities reward conformity and punish dissent. Only at the end of that chain does the state appear.

For this reason, counting executions or amputations alone cannot describe the full social impact of ḥudūd doctrine. A complete account must also consider the questions that were never asked, the doubts that were never spoken, the scholarship that was never pursued, the people who decided that silence was safer, and the families in which theological judgment entered relationships otherwise governed by love.

Human Dignity and the Freedom to Ask

The purpose of reform cannot therefore be merely to replace one punishment with another. Reform must restore the legitimacy of inquiry.

A Muslim must be able to ask whether a particular juristic interpretation is correct without first being required to defend his faith. He must be able to examine whether the evidentiary requirements of a ḥadd can ever be met safely under contemporary conditions. He must be able to ask whether an authoritarian government can be trusted with irreversible corporal punishment. He must be able to examine the distinction between revelation and later jurisprudence. He must be free to ask how the objectives of justice, mercy, proportionality, protection of the innocent, and human dignity should govern the interpretation and enforcement of criminal law.

These questions are not enemies of faith. They are questions about justice. And no system that claims to embody justice should fear examination.

The writer of Wujūb Taṭbīq al-Ḥudūd al-Sharʿiyya argues that the ḥudūd protect society through deterrence and that strict evidentiary conditions demonstrate the wisdom of the divine system. He also argues that crime should not be punished without first addressing social causes that may produce it, acknowledging poverty, exploitation, and social injustice as conditions that must be considered before enforcement. Those statements themselves open the door to questions the book does not pursue far enough.[50]

50ʿAbd al-Khāliq, Wujūb Taṭbīq al-Ḥudūd al-Sharʿiyya, 25–27. He emphasizes stringent proof requirements for zinā and theft and also argues that social causes of crime—including poverty, exploitation, and

What if the social conditions are unjust? What if poverty is widespread? What if political rulers are corrupt? What if police obtain confessions through coercion? What if courts are not independent? What if evidence is unreliable? What if the state selectively punishes the weak while protecting the powerful? What if an irreversible punishment is imposed and the judgment is later discovered to have been wrong?

At that point, the issue is no longer whether the believer accepts God. The issue is whether human institutions can be entrusted to claim God's authority over another human body. That question cannot be answered by calling the questioner an unbeliever.

What I Carried Away

When I left that family's home and returned to my hotel, I did not feel that I had won an argument. I felt brokenhearted.

I felt for the father. I felt for the son. I felt for the mother, who had maintained her composure and hospitality through an extraordinarily difficult day. I felt for the daughter, whose reaction came from the simple truth that she loved her brother. I had eaten their food, sat at their table, and witnessed something deeply painful unfolding among people who clearly belonged to one another.

I remember asking myself before God: Why must this happen? Why must faith become a place where a father believes that loyalty to God requires him to stand against the child he loves? Why should believers feel forced to choose between their conscience and what they have been told is an unquestionable interpretation of divine law?

I still believe these are legitimate questions. Perhaps they are among the most necessary questions we can ask.

The problem of the ḥudūd will not be resolved merely by comparing statutory provisions or collecting medieval juristic opinions. We must also examine the religious culture that has developed around those laws and the mechanisms through which certain interpretations have been protected from questioning.

Some of the most publicly influential guardians of the ḥudūd tradition are not necessarily its most accomplished jurists. They can be

---

failures of social solidarity—should be addressed before punishment is imposed.

writers, preachers, movements, institutions, and popular religious voices capable of translating complicated legal traditions into a simple choice between submission and unbelief. Their influence may depend less upon the sophistication of their jurisprudence than upon their ability to persuade believers that questioning a punishment means questioning God.

That is why a small book can matter. That is why a book I first read in Egypt could appear years later on a bedroom shelf in Europe. And that is why reform must begin before legislation.

It must begin by restoring the distinction between God and the human interpretation of God's will. It must begin by allowing the believer to ask questions without fear. It must begin by recognizing that conscience is not the enemy of faith, that compassion is not necessarily rebellion against God, and that human dignity cannot be protected where religious authority is permitted to place every legal interpretation beyond examination.

> *The power of the ḥudūd tradition does not begin when a judge pronounces a sentence. It begins much earlier, when the believer is taught that his own moral hesitation may have to be silenced in order to prove his obedience to God.*

Until that fear is confronted, legal reform alone will never be enough. The discussion can now return to the positive law itself. The next chapter begins with theft, where the distance between a punishment described as fixed and the human juristic construction required to activate it becomes especially clear.

Chapter Five

Theft, Property, and the Juristic Construction of Amputation

Among the ḥudūd, theft appears at first to provide the most direct connection between a clearly condemned act and an expressly stated punishment. The Qur'anic text refers to the male and female thief and commands the cutting of their hands. For defenders of the classical system, this seems to offer a particularly strong case for contemporary enforcement: property is indispensable to social order, theft is universally condemned, and the punishment is grounded in scriptural language. Aḥmad Fatḥī Bahnasi begins from this foundation. He defines theft subject to the ḥadd as the secret taking of property belonging to another person, of the required value, from protected custody, by a legally responsible offender, and without a recognized doubt of ownership or entitlement.[51]

That definition is revealing because the physical act of taking property is only the beginning of the legal inquiry. Before amputation becomes possible, the jurist must determine whether the property belonged entirely to another person, whether the taking was secret, whether the object was kept within legally sufficient protection, whether its value reached the required threshold, whether the accused possessed any claim, partnership, debt, family access, or other doubt, whether the object qualified as legally protected property, and whether necessity or social conditions affected responsibility. The punishment may be described as fixed, but the offense activating it is constructed through numerous disputed human judgments.

The chapter turns on a simple proposition:

> *Amputation is treated as a fixed punishment, while the legal definition of the theft that triggers it*

51Aḥmad Fatḥī Bahnasi, Al-Ḥudūd fī al-Islām (Alexandria: Mu'assasat Shabāb al-Jāmi'a, n.d.), 61–90, on sariqa and the conditions that distinguish technical ḥadd theft from other unlawful takings. See also Qur'an 5:38.

is assembled through contested juristic, economic, relational, and customary judgments.

The Technical Offense of Theft

Bahnasi distinguishes ḥadd theft from the wider moral category of taking property unlawfully. Fraud, breach of trust, embezzlement, open seizure, deception, extortion, unauthorized use, or failure to return entrusted property may remain sinful and punishable under taʿzīr, but they do not necessarily satisfy the technical conditions of sariqa. The distinction is understandable. Modern criminal law also differentiates theft, fraud, embezzlement, robbery, and breach of trust. Yet in Bahnasi's framework, classification determines not merely the legal name of the offense but whether the accused may lose a hand. The boundary between one property offense and another therefore carries an irreversible bodily consequence.[52]

Secrecy is one of the defining elements. The taking must be clandestine rather than openly forceful, a distinction that separates ordinary theft from robbery or ḥirāba. But the requirement immediately produces questions. What if access was initially lawful but the intention to keep the property arose later? What if an employee removes property from a place he is authorized to enter? What if funds are transferred electronically without physical entry? Classical doctrine developed around physically possessed objects and identifiable places of custody. Modern property may consist of digital funds, access credentials, data, electronic records, or intellectual assets. The moral wrong of unauthorized appropriation remains clear, but the technical category cannot simply be transferred without extensive reconstruction.

Ownership, Debt, and Relational Doubt

Bahnasi explains that the property must belong to another person. Where the accused possesses a genuine or legally significant claim, the resulting doubt may avert amputation. His discussion of public funds is

52Bahnasi distinguishes technical ḥadd theft from other unlawful takings that remain subject to taʿzīr. Compare the classical distinctions summarized in Mark A. Gabriel, "Reforming Hudud Ordinances to Reconcile Islamic Criminal Law with International Human Rights Law" (PhD diss., University of Cape Town, 2016), 101–4.

especially revealing. Some jurists decline amputation for theft from the public treasury because every Muslim is regarded as possessing a general interest in it; others allow amputation because no individual has authority to take public wealth without permission. The disagreement expresses two competing theories of public ownership. A modern legislature would have to select one of them before it could claim to enforce a fixed punishment.[53]

The public treasury example also exposes a troubling asymmetry. A poor person who steals privately owned property of the required value may face amputation, while an official who misappropriates public wealth may escape the ḥadd because the property is collectively owned, although discretionary punishment remains available. The distinction may follow the technical theory of ownership, but it does not necessarily correspond to the scale of social harm. It shows that the offense is organized around a particular property relationship rather than a proportional assessment of damage.

Debt creates a similar difficulty. Where a debtor takes from a creditor, or a creditor takes from a debtor, the claimed entitlement may establish sufficient doubt to prevent amputation. The court must then decide whether the debt exists, whether it is due, whether the amount taken exceeds the claim, and whether the accused sincerely or reasonably believed the property was owed. The corporal punishment therefore depends upon an ordinary human determination of contract, evidence, intention, and entitlement.

Bahnasi also records disagreement concerning theft between spouses, ascendants and descendants, relatives, servants, and others with lawful access. Marriage may preserve separate ownership, yet domestic access, maintenance obligations, or shared use may create doubt. A servant or employee may possess permission to enter the place where property is kept while lacking permission to take it. Family law, employment status, maintenance duties, and household practice thus become part of the criminal definition. A modern state choosing one classical position would not merely restore a punishment; it would adopt a historical theory of marriage, family access, and property relations.[54]

53Bahnasi, Al-Ḥudūd fī al-Islām, 61–90, on ownership doubt and theft from the public treasury.

The Minimum Value and the Problem of Proportionality

The minimum value, or niṣāb, is one of the best-known points of disagreement. The schools adopted different measures, including ten dirhams, three dirhams, and a quarter dinar. The threshold was intended to exclude trivial theft, but it creates a new legislative problem. Historical gold and silver values fluctuate, purchasing power changes, and modern currencies require conversion. A contemporary code would have to decide which school to follow, how to translate the threshold into present currency, whether to index it to inflation, and at what point the object should be valued. These are modern economic and legislative choices, not automatic consequences of revelation.[55]

A minimum threshold does not, by itself, create proportionality. It merely establishes a line below which amputation is unavailable. Once that line is crossed, the same permanent bodily punishment may apply to theft barely exceeding the threshold and to theft of very high value. The penalty does not rise gradually with the seriousness of the harm, nor does it permit full consideration of motive, planning, restitution, prior record, vulnerability of the victim, or the offender's role. The rigidity of the ḥadd appears most clearly at the point where formal completion replaces individualized judgment.

Protected Custody and Changing Custom

Another essential element is ḥirz, usually translated as protected custody or secure keeping. Property must generally be removed from a place or condition regarded as appropriate protection for that type of property. A house may protect household goods, a locked container may protect money, and a stable may protect animals. Yet the adequacy of custody depends heavily upon custom. What counts as secure varies by place, period, technology, occupation, and social expectation. Bahnasi's own analysis therefore demonstrates that a punishment presented as

54Bahnasi, Al-Ḥudūd fī al-Islām, 61–90, on theft between spouses, relatives, servants, and persons possessing lawful access.

55Gabriel, "Reforming Hudud Ordinances," 101–4. The dissertation records the differing thresholds adopted by the Ḥanafī, Mālikī, Shāfiʿī, and Ḥanbalī schools.

timeless depends for its activation upon a standard that changes with society.[56]

The requirement may be defended as limiting the ḥadd to serious intrusion, but it also makes the victim's protective conduct partly determinative. If the property was not adequately guarded, amputation may not apply, although taʿzīr remains possible. Modern law may reasonably treat forced entry as aggravating. It is far more difficult to justify making the irreversible loss of a hand depend upon contested judgments over whether a door, box, stable, workplace, electronic account, or storage system satisfied customary security.

The Nature of Property, Hunger, and Necessity

Bahnasi records disagreement over which objects qualify as protected property. Jurists considered whether the stolen object must be movable, durable, lawfully valuable, capable of private ownership, and recognized as wealth. Debates arose over food, crops, fruit, animals, books, religious texts, public property, prohibited items, and perishable goods. The moral wrong of taking another person's possession may be straightforward, but the juristic definition of qualifying property is not.[57]

The treatment of food becomes especially important where hunger is involved. Theft committed under deprivation cannot be separated morally from the conditions producing the deprivation. Bahnasi invokes the well-known report that ʿUmar suspended amputation during famine. The example is often presented as proof of mercy and contextual flexibility, and it certainly demonstrates both. But its deeper significance is that enforcement requires a political and socioeconomic judgment. The ruler or court must decide whether necessity exists, whether public failure has affected responsibility, and whether prevailing conditions make the punishment unjust.[58]

56Bahnasi, Al-Ḥudūd fī al-Islām, 61–90, on ḥirz and the role of custom in determining protected custody.

57Bahnasi, Al-Ḥudūd fī al-Islām, 61–90, on the kinds of property capable of supporting the ḥadd; Gabriel, "Reforming Hudud Ordinances," 49–50.

58Gabriel, "Reforming Hudud Ordinances," 193–94, citing the suspension of amputation during famine and arguing that necessity and

Necessity cannot be confined to a formally declared famine. Homelessness, unemployment, family hunger, medical need, coercion, mental impairment, debt, addiction, and lack of public assistance may all shape culpability. Legal capacity establishes that an adult of sound mind can be held responsible; it does not establish that amputation is proportionate in every circumstance. The traditional doctrine of doubt reduces the risk of punishment, but it cannot transform an irreversible penalty into an individualized response.

Proof, Victim Demand, and the State's Acquisition of the Case

Bahnasi places theft within the demanding evidentiary structure of the ḥudūd. Proof may arise through testimony or confession, and the wider doctrine encourages avoidance where doubt exists. These protections are important, but they reproduce the tension identified in earlier chapters: the punishment is treated as mandatory once established, while procedure is designed to prevent establishment in uncertain cases. The mercy lies largely in avoiding the sentence rather than in the sentence itself.[59]

Although theft is classified substantially as a right of God, some jurists require the owner to demand the property or initiate the claim before amputation may occur. The owner may possess information about permission, ownership, debt, or another doubt unknown to the court. The private right therefore re-enters the doctrine because the state cannot identify the offense without the victim's legal claim. The categories of divine and private rights are less separate in practice than they appear in theory.

Bahnasi also discusses the difference between forgiveness before and after referral to authority. Before the case reaches the ruler, the victim may forgive or decline to proceed. After formal referral and completion of proof, intercession is condemned and enforcement becomes obligatory. The underlying act, injury, property, and offender have not changed; what changes is the entry of the state. Once public authority takes possession of the case, the space for mercy contracts.

---

social reality require rejection of amputation in contemporary law.

59Bahnasi, Al-Ḥudūd fī al-Islām, 61–90, on proof by testimony or confession and the avoidance of ḥudūd in cases of doubt.

This is the sacralization described in Chapter Three in institutional form.[60]

Restitution, Amputation, and the Human Body

Jurists disagreed over whether the offender must return the property or pay compensation in addition to amputation. The disagreement reflects the mixed nature of the offense: amputation is treated as the right of God, while restitution protects the owner. From the victim's perspective, restitution is the more direct remedy. It repairs the economic loss as far as possible. Amputation does not restore the property, compensate the victim, or rebuild trust. Its function is symbolic, deterrent, and public rather than restorative.[61]

The classical jurists also debated the anatomical location of amputation and the treatment of repeated theft. The dominant view places the first amputation at the right wrist, while repeated offenses may lead, according to differing schools, to additional amputation or imprisonment. Such discussions display legal precision, but anatomical precision does not answer the moral question. Whether the hand is cut at the wrist or another joint, the authority intentionally creates permanent disability. Medical efforts to control bleeding or prevent death restrict the punishment to its intended form; they do not make mutilation compatible with dignity.[62]

The physical reality should not be hidden behind technical language. Amputation carries pain, blood loss, infection, shock, disability, psychological trauma, occupational loss, stigma, and lifelong social consequences. The authority is not merely applying an abstract ḥadd. It is destroying part of a human body. If a conviction is later shown to be mistaken, the body cannot be restored.

60Bahnasi, Al-Ḥudūd fī al-Islām, 61–90, on the prescribed amputation and juristic treatment of repeat theft.

61Bahnasi, Al-Ḥudūd fī al-Islām, 61–90, recording disagreements over thresholds, protected custody, ownership, access, necessity, and repeat offending.

62Bahnasi, Al-Ḥudūd fī al-Islām, 61–90; Gabriel, "Reforming Hudud Ordinances," 193–94, on necessity, famine, and the avoidance or suspension of amputation.

Deterrence, Selective Enforcement, and Irreversibility

The strongest defense of amputation is deterrence. The visible and permanent sentence is intended to frighten potential offenders and protect property. But deterrence cannot simply be presumed. A legitimate penal system must ask whether severity prevents theft more effectively than certainty of detection, whether poverty overrides fear, whether enforcement falls disproportionately upon the weak, whether victims avoid reporting because they do not wish to cause mutilation, and whether the punishment allows rehabilitation. A sentence does not become just merely because it is frightening.

The risk of unequal enforcement intensifies the problem. The wealthy may avoid prosecution through influence, officials may treat large-scale corruption as a discretionary offense, and the poor may be more visible to police and less able to obtain effective representation. Every criminal system faces such dangers, but the danger becomes intolerable where the sentence is irreversible. No evidentiary standard eliminates false testimony, mistaken identification, coerced confession, judicial error, fabricated documents, or later-discovered evidence. The doctrine of doubt may reduce risk; it cannot eliminate it.

The tension is now clear:

> *The more closely theft is defined, the less self-executing the punishment becomes.*

A modern legislature wishing to enforce amputation would have to create a new theft code. It would need to define digital property, electronic custody, joint marital ownership, employee access, public funds, debt claims, necessity, economic deprivation, confession, restitution, and repeated offenses. The final penalty might resemble the classical rule, but the operative offense would be a modern political construction.

A Constructive Alternative

Rejecting amputation does not weaken protection of property. Theft should remain a serious criminal offense, and victims should receive restitution, compensation, protection against future loss, and efficient access to justice. A modern system can distinguish necessity, first offenses, repeated professional theft, organized crime, corruption, breach of trust, violence, and restitution. It may use graduated fines, community supervision, rehabilitation, treatment, employment support, and imprisonment where necessary. Such a system can impose stronger penalties for large-scale corruption and organized economic crime than for minor theft committed under deprivation.

This approach is not moral permissiveness. It preserves the Qur'anic concern for property, accountability, and social trust while separating that concern from permanent bodily mutilation. Your earlier doctoral work already moved in this direction by proposing imprisonment and/or financial penalties, with the value of the property and circumstances of the offense taken into account. The present book carries that development further: alternative punishment is not merely a temporary reform of the ḥadd. It reflects the conclusion that amputation should stand outside the lawful authority of the modern state.[63]

63Gabriel, "Reforming Hudud Ordinances," 193–94, proposing imprisonment and/or a fine according to the value of the property and the circumstances of the offense; see also 198–99 on replacing corporal punishment with individualized taʿzīr penalties.

Conclusion

Bahnasi's treatment of theft is detailed and intellectually important. It shows that classical jurists did not impose amputation for every act casually described as stealing. They required secrecy, qualifying property, protected custody, minimum value, legal capacity, and the absence of ownership doubt. They examined debt, spouses, relatives, servants, public property, necessity, famine, restitution, repeated offenses, and evidentiary uncertainty. These doctrines demonstrate legal sophistication. They also establish the case against contemporary enforcement.

The supposedly fixed offense is composed of disputed historical, customary, economic, and relational judgments. The punishment becomes certain only after fallible institutions have made numerous uncertain decisions. The law does not discover one self-evident act called theft and then apply an automatic divine sentence. It constructs a technical offense through human jurisprudence and attaches irreversible bodily injury to that construction.

Theft should remain punishable, property should be protected, and victims should receive justice. But no state, regime, or armed movement claiming to enforce Islamic criminal law should amputate a human hand on the basis of contested judgments concerning value, custody, ownership, custom, necessity, and doubt. The next chapter turns from property crime to public violence and the doctrine of ḥirāba.

Chapter Six

Ḥirāba, Public Violence, and Punishment as Spectacle

The offense of ḥirāba occupies a distinctive place within classical Islamic criminal law. Unlike ordinary theft, it is not defined primarily by secrecy. It concerns the open use or threat of force against persons, property, movement, and public security. Aḥmad Fatḥī Bahnasi describes it as the "greater theft," distinguishing it from ordinary theft because its harm extends beyond one victim to roads, travelers, commerce, and the wider community. The Qur'anic passage upon which the doctrine rests refers to those who wage war against God and His Messenger and strive to spread corruption in the land. It lists killing, crucifixion, cutting hands and feet from opposite sides, and banishment, while making a distinction for repentance before capture.[64]

The conduct at issue may be exceptionally serious. Armed robbery, murder, kidnapping, organized violence, and terrorizing travelers plainly justify a strong criminal-law response. The question is not whether such conduct should be punished. It is whether the inherited categories and punishments provide a sufficiently precise, proportionate, and constitutionally safe framework for a modern state. The same pattern found in theft appears here with even greater force: the punishment is presented as revealed and fixed, while the offense is defined through contested judgments about place, weapons, coercive power, gender, status, participation, property, repentance, and political authority.

The argument is straightforward:

> *The classical law of ḥirāba identifies grave and genuine social harms, but joins contested*

64 Qur'an 5:33–34; Aḥmad Fatḥī Bahnasi, Al-Ḥudūd fī al-Islām (Alexandria: Mu'assasat Shabāb al-Jāmi'a, n.d.), section on ḥirāba. For the overlapping classical definitions of ḥirāba, qaṭ' al-ṭarīq, and baghy and their relation to Qur'an 5:33, see Gabriel, "Reforming Hudud Ordinances," 93–95.

definitions to irreversible punishment and public spectacle.

From Theft to Public Terror

Bahnasi distinguishes ḥirāba from ordinary theft by the manner and social effect of the conduct. Ordinary theft is secret; ḥirāba is open, forceful, and intimidating. The offender confronts persons, blocks movement, displays power, and produces fear. The protected interests include life, bodily security, property, freedom of movement, commercial activity, the safety of roads, and confidence in public order. This wider harm explains why jurists treated the offense more severely than ordinary theft. It is not simply aggravated property crime; it is an assault upon the community's ability to move and live without terror.[65]

The Qur'anic language of "waging war against God and His Messenger" and "corruption in the land" gives the offense extraordinary moral force. Within its historical setting, the language communicates the gravity of organized violence against the community. In the hands of a modern government, however, the same language may become dangerously expansive. A state may begin with armed robbery and murder, then extend "war against God" or "corruption in the land" to political opposition, protest, dissident speech, religious disagreement, economic misconduct, or civil unrest. Criminal law requires precision, especially where execution, crucifixion, or mutilation is possible. The accused should not face irreversible punishment under a concept whose limits depend upon the moral and political judgment of the authority prosecuting the case.

Place, Weapons, and Coercive Capacity

Bahnasi records disagreement over where ḥirāba may occur. Some jurists connect it primarily to roads and places beyond immediate governmental protection, where travelers are isolated and unable to obtain assistance. Others extend the offense to cities where armed groups can produce the same fear and public danger. Abū Ḥanīfa is

---

65 Bahnasi, Al-Ḥudūd fī al-Islām, section on ḥirāba, describing the offense in relation to public fear, roads, life, and property; see also Gabriel, "Reforming Hudud Ordinances," 93–95, on the overlapping classical definitions of ḥirāba, highway robbery, and rebellion.

presented as taking a narrower position concerning inhabited areas, while Mālik and others permit a broader application. The disagreement is consequential because geography may determine whether the same act is treated as robbery, murder, assault, theft, or ḥirāba carrying the severest penalties.[66]

The dispute reflects historical conditions. Classical cities often possessed guards, neighbors, markets, and concentrated authority, while rural roads exposed travelers to a distinct danger. Modern violence does not respect that geography. It may occur in a city, on a highway, inside a home, in public transportation, through an organized gang, or across borders. A modern legal system should classify conduct according to violence, coercion, organization, intent, and harm rather than inherited assumptions about where security is ordinarily available.

Jurists also disagreed over whether weapons are required. Some connected the offense to armed force; others focused more broadly upon the actual capacity to intimidate and overpower, whether through weapons, physical strength, numbers, or other means. Contemporary coercion may involve vehicles, explosives, chemical substances, kidnapping, threats against relatives, digital control of infrastructure, coordinated numbers, or the apparent possession of a weapon. A modern legislature would therefore have to reconstruct the classical category by creating a new definition of force.[67]

Status, Gender, and Individual Responsibility

Bahnasi records disagreement over whether women may be treated as perpetrators of ḥirāba and whether free and enslaved persons stand under the same rule. These disagreements reveal the social assumptions and hierarchy within which the doctrine developed. Where the offense concerns violence, killing, terror, and seizure of property, sex or

---

66 Bahnasi, Al-Ḥudūd fī al-Islām, section on ḥirāba, recording disagreement over the territorial setting of the offense. See also Gabriel, "Reforming Hudud Ordinances," 93–95, for the broader definitional disagreement surrounding ḥirāba and qaṭʿ al-ṭarīq.

67 Bahnasi, Al-Ḥudūd fī al-Islām, section on ḥirāba, on weapons or sufficient force to overpower and intimidate; see also Gabriel, "Reforming Hudud Ordinances," 93–95, on the classical association of the offense with force, public fear, robbery, and violence.

inherited status should not determine criminal classification. A modern constitutional system must begin from equal legal personhood and evaluate conduct rather than historical expectations concerning gender or freedom.[68]

Legal capacity remains necessary: the accused must generally be adult and sane. Yet those requirements do not settle whether the person acted voluntarily, whether he or she was a principal or subordinate, whether participation occurred under coercion, whether violence was intended, whether the person knew the group's purpose, or whether withdrawal occurred before the offense. These distinctions become indispensable where punishment may include death or mutilation.

Ḥirāba is often committed by a group, and group cases intensify the problem of individual responsibility. One person may carry a weapon, another restrain the victim, another take property, another kill, and another stand at a distance as a lookout. One participant may join the group but attempt to prevent the killing. A modern criminal code must distinguish principals, accomplices, conspirators, aiders, coerced participants, and persons who withdraw. Collective membership cannot substitute for proof of individual culpability.

The Graduated Forms of the Offense

Bahnasi presents the familiar graduated structure: killing combined with taking property may lead to killing and crucifixion; killing without taking property may lead to execution, with disagreement over crucifixion; taking property without killing may lead to cross-amputation; terrorizing travelers without killing or taking property may lead to banishment; and repentance before capture may remove the public ḥadd while preserving private rights. The structure attempts to connect greater harm with greater punishment. That principle is reasonable. The penalties selected to express it remain deeply problematic.[69]

---

68 Bahnasi, Al-Ḥudūd fī al-Islām, section on ḥirāba, recording disagreements concerning female offenders and enslaved persons. For the wider problem of status-based distinctions within the ḥudūd, see Gabriel, "Reforming Hudud Ordinances," 99–100, 124–26.

69 Qur'an 5:33; Bahnasi, Al-Ḥudūd fī al-Islām, section on ḥirāba, on the differentiated penalties associated with killing, property-taking,

Where killing and property-taking occur together, crucifixion adds something beyond incapacitation or retribution. It adds public display, humiliation, warning, and spectacle. The body becomes an instrument through which authority communicates power. All punishment has a communicative element, but crucifixion makes that communication physically extreme. It does not merely remove a dangerous person; it stages the body as a warning to others.

This is exemplary punishment in its most literal form. The suffering and displayed body of the condemned person become a means to influence the public. The moral question is not whether the crime was grave. It is whether government may deliberately degrade a human body to produce fear. A commitment to dignity cannot disappear at conviction or death.

Cross-Amputation and Banishment

Where property is taken without killing, Bahnasi presents cross-amputation: removal of the right hand and left foot. The body is made to symbolize the structure of the offense, with the hand associated with taking and the opposite foot added because of open force and disruption of public security. Symbolism does not establish proportionality. Cross-amputation creates permanent impairment, loss of mobility and employment, chronic pain, psychological trauma, dependence, and lifelong exclusion. The punishment reorganizes the offender's entire bodily future.[70]

Bahnasi also records disagreement over whether the property must reach the niṣāb required in ordinary theft and whether it must have been within protected custody. Some jurists carry those requirements into ḥirāba; others regard force and terror as sufficient. A small amount of property may therefore trigger cross-amputation under one opinion and not another. The difference between lifelong disability and another

---

intimidation, banishment, and repentance before capture. See also Gabriel, "Reforming Hudud Ordinances," 49–50, 196–99.

70Mark A. Gabriel, "Reforming Hudud Ordinances to Reconcile Islamic Criminal Law with International Human Rights Law" (PhD diss., University of Cape Town, 2016), 49–50, 196–99, discussing the Qur'anic penalties for ḥirāba and proposing alternative punishments compatible with human-rights standards.

sentence depends upon which juristic construction the modern authority chooses.

For intimidation without killing or taking property, the prescribed response is banishment or exile. Yet banishment itself is disputed. It may mean removal from a place, imprisonment, pursuit, exclusion from an area, or some other form of restriction. Modern law would have to decide whether it means imprisonment, internal exile, deportation, relocation, travel restrictions, or exclusion from a region. None of these is a self-evident implementation of the Qur'anic expression, and some may conflict with citizenship, nationality rights, family life, and international obligations.[71]

Fixed Correspondence or Judicial Choice

The Qur'anic verse lists several punishments with the conjunction "or." Jurists disagreed over whether each punishment corresponds automatically to a particular form of the offense or whether the ruler or judge possesses broader discretion to choose among them according to circumstances. This is a foundational interpretive question. If the punishments are tied rigidly to outcomes, the system appears fixed. If the ruler may choose, substantial political discretion enters the punishment. Either way, interpretation remains indispensable.[72]

Repentance Before Capture

One of the most important features of the doctrine is repentance before capture. Bahnasi explains that repentance before the authorities gain control may remove the public ḥadd, while private rights remain. The offender may still owe retaliation for killing or injury, restitution, compensation, or other consequences belonging to victims. The

---

71 Bahnasi, Al-Ḥudūd fī al-Islām, section on ḥirāba, on the disputed meaning of banishment; see also Gabriel, "Reforming Hudud Ordinances," 49–50, 196–99, on Qur'an 5:33 and reform of the classical penalties.

72 The juristic disagreement concerns whether the conjunction in Qur'an 5:33 indicates a correspondence between particular offenses and punishments or grants the ruler a measure of choice. For the broader disagreement surrounding ḥirāba and its punishments, see Gabriel, "Reforming Hudud Ordinances," 49–50, 93–95, 196–99.

distinction is morally important because spiritual repentance cannot erase bodily injury, economic loss, or the claims of the family of the dead.[73]

The rule also contains a constructive practical insight. It encourages offenders to abandon violence, surrender, return property, stop endangering the public, and prevent further bloodshed. Yet it creates a sharp temporal boundary. A person who commits grave violence and repents before capture may escape the public ḥadd; another who experiences the same moral change after capture may face execution, crucifixion, or cross-amputation. The difference may be hours or chance. What changes is not necessarily repentance but the state's possession of the offender.

Modern law can preserve the constructive purpose without an all-or-nothing distinction. Surrender, return of property, rescue of victims, disclosure of weapons, cooperation, and prevention of further crimes may justify transparent and reviewable mitigation. Such mitigation should respect victims' rights and individualized culpability rather than depend entirely upon whether capture occurred first.

The Boundary with Rebellion and Terrorism

Ḥirāba is especially attractive to political authorities because it joins criminal violence with theological defense of public order. The state may claim not merely to protect citizens and roads but to suppress war against God and corruption in the land. That language may strengthen legitimate action against violent groups, but it also expands the government's interpretive power over security, corruption, rebellion, terror, and divine order.

The boundary between ḥirāba and baghy, or rebellion, is not always clear. The highway robber may seek private gain, while the rebel claims political or religious justification and opposes the ruler through organized force. Yet violent movements may combine ideology, territorial control, attacks on civilians, property seizure, and opposition to government. Classification then becomes political. Calling the group rebels may preserve certain protections; calling them muḥāribūn may

---

73 Qur'an 5:34; Bahnasi, Al-Ḥudūd fī al-Islām, section on ḥirāba, on repentance before capture and the survival of victims' private claims; see also Gabriel, "Reforming Hudud Ordinances," 196–99.

expose them to crucifixion or cross-amputation. The state's power to classify becomes the power to determine the body's fate.[74]

Ḥirāba also overlaps with modern terrorism but is not identical to it. Both may involve public fear, organized violence, and attacks upon persons and property. Modern terrorism law, however, often requires political, ideological, or coercive purposes and may reach conduct far beyond highway robbery. Direct transplantation of ḥirāba into antiterrorism law could therefore broaden criminal liability dangerously. Ordinary criminal statutes can punish murder, attempted murder, armed robbery, kidnapping, conspiracy, assault, extortion, destruction of property, organized crime, and terrorism without crucifixion or mutilation.

Punishment as Spectacle and the Danger of State Power

The severity of the conduct does not automatically legitimate every severe response. Murder, armed robbery, and terror may justify long imprisonment and secure incapacitation. They do not make crucifixion, cross-amputation, or public degradation proportionate. Punishment must remain necessary, individualized, reviewable, non-discriminatory, and compatible with dignity.

Public punishment communicates sovereignty as well as justice. The crucified body declares that authority has defeated the person who challenged public order. Under authoritarian government, the theatrical dimension becomes especially dangerous. The accused may be presented not merely as a criminal but as an enemy of God, and punishment may become a performance of political domination.

Fear is not the same as justice. Spectacular punishment may frighten potential offenders, but it may also produce silence, false confession, political submission, concealment, and public desensitization to violence. A just state should seek confidence in lawful institutions, not terror of government.

---

74 Bahnasi, Al-Ḥudūd fī al-Islām, sections on ḥirāba and al-baghy. For the close overlap among ḥirāba, qaṭʿ al-ṭarīq, and rebellion in classical doctrine, see Gabriel, "Reforming Hudud Ordinances," 93–95.

Irreversibility and Group Prosecution

All the evidentiary risks identified in theft remain present in ḥirāba, but the consequences are greater. A court may err concerning identity, group membership, possession of a weapon, participation in killing, intention, value of property, repentance, or completion of the offense. A wrongful prison sentence may later be corrected only imperfectly; a wrongful execution, crucifixion, or cross-amputation cannot be corrected at all.

Group prosecutions often arise during unstable political conditions. Evidence may come from accomplices, security services, emergency courts, intelligence reports, coerced confessions, or politically interested witnesses. The closer the case lies to national security, the greater the danger that ordinary safeguards will be weakened. Sacralizing punishment magnifies that danger because political judgment is presented as enforcement of divine order.

A Constructive Modern Approach

The legitimate purposes associated with ḥirāba should be preserved: protection of roads and public spaces, security of travelers, protection of life and property, suppression of organized violence, victim compensation, encouragement of surrender, and prevention of repeated harm. A modern system can pursue these purposes through precise statutes, individualized liability, fair trial, restitution, proportionate imprisonment, witness protection, secure incapacitation where necessary, rehabilitation where possible, and reviewable sentence reduction for genuine cooperation.

Gabriel's earlier doctoral research already proposed replacing the classical corporal and capital penalties for ḥirāba with imprisonment calibrated to the seriousness and circumstances of the offense. It also emphasized that imprisonment can deter, incapacitate, and permit rehabilitation while reducing the ability of rulers to use death and mutilation against opponents. The present book advances that position by concluding that crucifixion and cross-amputation should not remain within the lawful authority of any modern state, regime, or armed movement claiming to enforce Islamic criminal law.[75]

75Gabriel, "Reforming Hudud Ordinances," 196–99, arguing for imprisonment rather than crucifixion, amputation, or execution and

Conclusion

Bahnasi's treatment of ḥirāba reflects a serious effort to distinguish degrees of public violence. It differentiates killing with property-taking, killing without property-taking, property-taking without killing, intimidation without either, and repentance before capture. It also preserves private rights even where the public ḥadd falls. These distinctions show an attempt to connect punishment with the gravity of conduct.

Yet the doctrine remains deeply dependent upon juristic construction. Jurists disagree over city and countryside, weapons, gender, free and enslaved status, individual participation, property thresholds, protected custody, crucifixion, banishment, judicial choice, and the effect of repentance. At the same time, the possible sentences include execution, public display, and permanent bodily mutilation.

A modern state should punish murder, armed robbery, kidnapping, organized violence, and terror with great seriousness. But it should not crucify, cross-amputate, or sacralize its own violence by describing the accused as one who wages war against God. The purpose of law should be to restore security, protect victims, and restrain dangerous offenders —not to convert the human body into a public warning. The next chapter turns from public violence to private sexual morality and the law of zinā.

---

emphasizing the danger of rulers using ḥirāba against political opposition.

Chapter Seven

Zinā, Stoning, and the Criminalization of Private Morality

The classical law of zinā presents one of the sharpest conflicts between religious morality and the coercive authority of the state. Theft and ḥirāba involve identifiable injuries to property, bodily security, and public safety. Zinā, by contrast, may involve private sexual conduct between consenting adults where no force, fraud, exploitation, or direct physical injury to another person has occurred. This does not make the conduct morally insignificant. Within Islamic teaching, sexual relations outside lawful marriage carry serious religious and social meaning. They may involve betrayal, family disruption, broken trust, disputed parentage, emotional injury, and abandonment of responsibility. A religious community may therefore teach chastity, fidelity, repentance, and family obligation with great seriousness. The central question is different: does the moral prohibition of zinā justify giving a modern state authority to investigate private intimacy, flog human bodies, or kill by stoning?

Bahnasi's discussion demonstrates that the answer cannot be derived from one simple and undisputed penal rule. His account depends upon the technical definition of penetration, the legal status of iḥṣān, four eyewitnesses, confession, pregnancy, disputed forms of sexual conduct, flogging, exile, stoning, and the reported "verse of stoning," whose recitation is said to have disappeared while its ruling remained. The doctrinal complexity is extraordinary, yet the consequence may be death.

The Technical Construction of Zinā

Bahnasi defines zinā as unlawful sexual intercourse under specified conditions and then presents a more technical juristic formulation centered upon penetration without valid marriage, lawful entitlement, or a legally recognized ambiguity. The definition establishes a narrow threshold, but it also requires intimate factual and legal judgments. The court must determine the degree of penetration, whether the parties believed a marriage existed, whether a defective marriage created shubha, whether coercion or incapacity was present, whether the accused understood the legal status of the relationship, and whether any recognized doubt prevented the ḥadd.[76][77]

The state's entry into this field is therefore invasive by its nature. Police, prosecutors, judges, witnesses, and religious authorities may be drawn into bedrooms, marital records, prior marriages, divorce dates, pregnancy, confession, and the precise character of sexual contact. Criminalizing private sexual morality grants government power over one of the most intimate areas of human life. The investigation itself may violate privacy and dignity before guilt is ever established.

Sin, Harm, and Public Crime

A legal system must distinguish conduct considered sinful from conduct that should be prosecuted as a crime. Not every moral wrong belongs within penal law. A person may betray trust, lie within a relationship, neglect religious obligations, or cause emotional pain without becoming subject to corporal punishment. Moral condemnation does not by itself establish that the state should investigate, expose, imprison, flog, or kill.

The law must also distinguish consensual relations from rape, coercion, trafficking, exploitation, abuse of children, and abuse of

---

76 Bahnasi, Al-Ḥudūd fī al-Islām, section on zinā, on the technical definition of intercourse, valid marriage, and shubha. For the classical definitions, proof requirements, and school disagreements, see Gabriel, "Reforming Hudud Ordinances," 95–100.

77 Qur'an 24:2; Aḥmad Fatḥī Bahnasi, Al-Ḥudūd fī al-Islām (Alexandria: Mu'assasat Shabāb al-Jāmi'a, n.d.), section on zinā. See also Gabriel, "Reforming Hudud Ordinances," 95–100, on the classical distinction between married and unmarried offenders and the corresponding penalties.

authority. The traditional category is organized principally around lawful or unlawful intercourse; modern criminal law must begin with consent and harm. Sexual violence attacks bodily autonomy and may require severe punishment. Consensual zinā may violate religious teaching or marital responsibility, but it does not involve the same injury. A legal order that fails to center consent risks confusing moral disapproval with protection against violence.

Iḥṣān and the Boundary Between Flogging and Death

Bahnasi explains that punishment changes according to iḥṣān. The person classified as muḥṣan faces stoning, while the non-muḥṣan faces one hundred lashes, with additional disagreement over exile. In penal doctrine, iḥṣān becomes a status based chiefly upon prior valid marital intercourse, together with requirements developed by the jurists. The difference is absolute: one person is flogged; another is killed. The sexual act may be identical. The difference lies in legal biography.[78]

The status may continue after a marriage ends. Two unmarried adults may therefore commit the same act at the same time, yet one may be flogged because he or she has never consummated a valid marriage while the other may be stoned because of a marriage that ended years earlier. The punishment is not proportioned solely to present conduct, present harm, or present family circumstances. It is determined partly by past marital history.

The conditions of iḥṣān are themselves disputed. Jurists differed over adulthood, sanity, freedom, Islam, valid marriage, consummation, and the manner in which the status is proven. Islamic jurisprudence also distinguishes valid, irregular, void, and mistaken marriages. These distinctions may avert punishment through shubha, but they also show that the boundary between flogging and death depends upon technical family-law interpretation. A human being should not live or die because a court selected one juristic theory of marriage over another.

---

78 Bahnasi, Al-Ḥudūd fī al-Islām, section on zinā, on iḥṣān and the distinction between the muḥṣan and non-muḥṣan offender; Gabriel, "Reforming Hudud Ordinances," 95–97.

Four Witnesses, Concealment, and Privacy

Bahnasi states that zinā may be proven by four qualified eyewitnesses who directly observe the act and agree concerning its essential circumstances. The rule makes conviction through testimony exceptionally difficult and may be understood as a barrier against rumor, suspicion, reputation, or circumstantial intimacy. It protects privacy and communicates that concealed sexual wrongdoing should not be exposed casually.[79]

Yet the rule creates an internal contradiction. If private zinā should remain concealed and proof requires observation so explicit that conviction is nearly impossible, then the substantive punishment appears designed for conduct that has become effectively public. The procedural structure seeks to keep the punishment unreachable. Once again, mercy lies in avoiding the sentence rather than in the sentence itself.

The act of witnessing may itself require intrusion into a private space and deliberate observation of nakedness. Bahnasi records juristic concern over whether witnesses who intentionally look compromise their own moral standing. The state demands morally qualified witnesses, but obtaining the required knowledge may itself involve a violation of privacy. Disagreement over delayed testimony, contradictions among witnesses, and the judge's personal knowledge further demonstrates that the evidentiary route to capital punishment was never uniform.

Bahnasi strongly emphasizes satr, the concealment of private wrongdoing. This is one of the most humane features of his account. But it supports a conclusion more far-reaching than the classical doctrine draws: where conduct is private and consensual, religious teaching, pastoral counsel, marital remedies, repentance, and personal accountability are more consistent with concealment than criminal prosecution. The criminal court is an institution of exposure.

---

79 Bahnasi, Al-Ḥudūd fī al-Islām, section on zinā, on proof by four witnesses, agreement among witnesses, and concealment of private wrongdoing. See Gabriel, "Reforming Hudud Ordinances," 98–100, on confession, four male eyewitnesses, direct observation, and disagreement over testimony.

Confession, Retraction, and Psychological Vulnerability

Because four-witness proof is so difficult, confession becomes central to the historical cases. Bahnasi records disagreement over whether one confession is sufficient or whether four separate admissions are required. The reported authorities turn away, question the confessor, investigate sanity, and permit repeated opportunities for reconsideration. That reluctance deserves recognition. It also raises a deeper question: why should a modern state preserve a punishment whose most merciful administration requires repeated efforts to prevent a willing confessor from reaching it?[80]

Jurists also disagreed over retraction. Some accept withdrawal even after punishment begins because it creates doubt; others regard a valid confession as establishing the ḥadd. The dispute determines whether the state must stop killing a person who no longer maintains the confession upon which the sentence rests. Capital punishment cannot rest securely upon disputed rules of retraction.

A confession may arise from mental illness, depression, overwhelming shame, coercion, family pressure, a desire for religious purification, fear of the afterlife, or a wish to die. Premodern inquiries into sanity could not supply modern psychiatric assessment. Government should not transform religious guilt into a pathway toward state-assisted death.

Pregnancy and Unequal Enforcement

Pregnancy is another disputed evidentiary issue. Some Mālikī reasoning may treat unexplained pregnancy in an unmarried woman as evidence of zinā, subject to possible explanations such as coercion or mistake. Other jurists reject pregnancy alone as sufficient because it may arise from rape, mistaken intercourse, or another legally relevant doubt.[81]

---

80 Bahnasi, Al-Ḥudūd fī al-Islām, section on zinā, on confession, the number of admissions, and retraction. See Gabriel, "Reforming Hudud Ordinances," 98–100, 188–90, on confession, evidentiary thresholds, and withdrawal of confession.

81 Bahnasi, Al-Ḥudūd fī al-Islām, section on zinā, on pregnancy as disputed evidence; see also Gabriel, "Reforming Hudud Ordinances," 98–100, 183–90.

The inequality is structural. The man's participation may remain hidden, while the woman's pregnancy cannot. Her body becomes evidence against her, and she may bear the burden of explaining what occurred in private. A pregnant woman may have been raped, coerced, trafficked, threatened, or unable to resist. A consent-centered legal system must begin by protecting the possible victim, not presuming sexual guilt from pregnancy.

Disputed Sexual Conduct and Juristic Classification

Bahnasi discusses payment to a woman followed by intercourse, presenting the juristic question whether payment creates a resemblance to marital entitlement sufficient to establish shubha. The discussion reveals how technical legal reasoning may obscure exploitation and how the boundary among prostitution, irregular contract, and zinā depended upon juristic theory. Modern law should ask whether there was consent, exploitation, trafficking, deception, or abuse of economic desperation rather than whether payment resembles mahr.

He also records profound disagreement over same-sex conduct and other sexual acts. Some jurists leave male same-sex conduct to taʿzīr, others analogize it to zinā, and still others advocate death, with further disagreement over method and marital status. The variation is incompatible with the claim that one clear and self-executing divine penalty exists. A modern authority selecting death from among these opinions would be making a human political choice.[82]

The Qur'anic Text and the Doctrine of Stoning

The Qur'anic verse prescribes one hundred lashes for the female and male offender. Its wording does not expressly distinguish married from unmarried offenders. The later division rests upon iḥṣān, Sunnah reports, historical practice, and juristic interpretation. Bahnasi records major disagreement over whether the muḥṣan receives stoning alone, flogging and stoning together, or whether flogging remains the

---

82 Bahnasi, Al-Ḥudūd fī al-Islām, section on zinā, on disputed sexual acts and differing juristic classifications and punishments. See also Gabriel, "Reforming Hudud Ordinances," 95–100.

punishment for all. There is also disagreement over exile after flogging. The law determining life or death is therefore not uniform.[83]

The reported "verse of stoning" presents the greatest textual difficulty. Bahnasi explains the classical claim that its recitation was removed while its legal ruling remained, a doctrine known as abrogation of recitation with survival of the ruling. The proposition is extraordinary: a capital punishment is maintained through words no longer found in the Qur'an, on the theory that God removed their recitation but preserved their legal force.[84]

Bahnasi does not ignore the objections. He discusses why the reported text was not included in the written Qur'an, the concern that ʿUmar might be accused of adding to the Book of God, and explanations for retaining the judgment after removal of the words. The need for such explanations confirms that the textual foundation is not simple. In a modern penal system, especially one imposing death, the governing rule should be accessible, clear, and publicly verifiable.

The extant Qur'an states flogging. Stoning depends upon reports of prophetic practice, an omitted verse, theories of abrogation, chronology, and consensus claims. Whatever theological weight those materials may carry, they do not possess the same public clarity as an existing Qur'anic penal text. A modern state should not kill where the relationship among the sources remains historically and juristically reconstructed.

Stoning, Flogging, and Punishment as Spectacle

Bahnasi defines stoning as killing the muḥṣan offender through repeated throwing of stones until death. He discusses who begins the punishment and differences between convictions based on confession and testimony. Requiring witnesses to cast the first stones may be

---

83 Qur'an 24:2; Bahnasi, Al-Ḥudūd fī al-Islām, section on zinā, on flogging, stoning, exile, and differing positions concerning the muḥṣan offender; Gabriel, "Reforming Hudud Ordinances," 95–98, 183–86.

84 Bahnasi, Al-Ḥudūd fī al-Islām, section on zinā, discussing the reported verse of stoning and the doctrine of abrogation of recitation while retaining the ruling. For the broader textual controversy surrounding stoning, see Gabriel, "Reforming Hudud Ordinances," 183 –86.

presented as a final test of certainty, but truth should be tested through evidence, cross-examination, corroboration, and judicial scrutiny—not by making accusers participants in execution.[85]

Stoning is not an instantaneous death. It is a collective process in which repeated blows injure the body until life ends. Public or communal participation distributes responsibility and may weaken individual moral accountability. The same tradition that prefers concealment turns the convicted body into a public lesson.

For the non-muḥṣan, Bahnasi presents one hundred lashes. Jurists regulate the instrument, force, distribution of blows, clothing, bodily areas, illness, pregnancy, and postponement. Such rules seek to prevent death or excessive injury, but regulated flogging remains intentional bodily violence. Technical moderation does not answer whether government should whip a consenting adult for private sexual conduct.

Marriage, Injury, and the Limits of Penal Repair

Adultery may create identifiable victims. A spouse may suffer betrayal, emotional injury, financial loss, exposure to disease, disputed parentage, or marital breakdown. Those harms are real. Yet the injured spouse does not necessarily benefit from the state flogging or killing the other spouse. The family may need divorce remedies, financial protection, custody rules, medical care, compensation where appropriate, and privacy. Corporal punishment may deepen rather than repair the injury.

Fidelity is a moral and relational commitment. It may be strengthened through character, religious teaching, family responsibility, mutual respect, and enforceable civil obligations. Fear of flogging or stoning may produce concealment; it cannot create love, trust, or genuine faithfulness.

Plural Citizenship and the Constitutional Problem

A modern state contains citizens of different religions, interpretations, and convictions. If zinā is punished because Islamic law prohibits it, the government must decide whether the law applies to non-Muslims,

---

85 Bahnasi, Al-Ḥudūd fī al-Islām, section on zinā, on the procedure of stoning and participation in its execution; see also Gabriel, "Reforming Hudud Ordinances," 97–100, 183–86.

mixed-faith couples, civil marriages, marriages valid under another religion, and citizens who do not accept the governing school's definition of iḥṣān. The doctrine cannot be transferred into a plural constitutional order without profound inequality.[86]

Removing consensual zinā from criminal law does not mean sexual conduct becomes immune from accountability. The law should punish rape, coercion, trafficking, child abuse, exploitation, harassment, abuse of authority, nonconsensual recording, and intentional transmission of serious harm. It may regulate the civil consequences of marital betrayal. The distinction is not between morality and chaos. It is between protecting persons from harm and policing private consensual sin.

A Constructive Alternative

The moral purposes associated with the prohibition can be preserved without corporal or capital punishment. A modern framework may protect against sexual violence, apply equal standards of consent, protect children, punish exploitation and trafficking, provide civil remedies for marital breakdown, enforce financial responsibility toward spouses and children, preserve confidential medical care, and protect privacy. Religious communities may continue to teach chastity, fidelity, repentance, and reconciliation. The state should not flog or stone.

Gabriel's earlier doctoral research already argued that the classical justifications for stoning were too weak to sustain such a severe punishment and concluded that stoning should not be practiced. It also proposed replacing ḥadd punishments with individualized taʿzīr responses compatible with human-rights standards. The present study moves further by concluding that private consensual sexual morality should stand outside corporal and capital state enforcement altogether.[87]

86For the modern transformation of plural juristic doctrine into centralized state law, see Wael B. Hallaq, Shari'a: Theory, Practice, Transformations (Cambridge: Cambridge University Press, 2009), 357–443.

87Gabriel, 'Reforming Hudud Ordinances,' 183–99, arguing against stoning and for alternative punishments compatible with human-rights standards.

Conclusion

Bahnasi's treatment of zinā displays both juristic sophistication and internal strain. The jurists narrowly define the physical act, require extraordinary proof, recognize doubt, prefer concealment, and debate confession, retraction, pregnancy, defective marriage, iḥṣān, exile, flogging, and stoning. These protections and disagreements reveal sustained legal reflection. They also reveal that the offense is not self-executing.

The deepest contradiction is this:

> *The procedural law seeks privacy. The substantive law destroys the body.*

A modern state should resolve that contradiction not by refining the mechanics of flogging or narrowing the circumstances of stoning, but by removing consensual sexual morality from corporal and capital criminal enforcement. Zinā may remain a religious and moral prohibition. Adultery may remain a grave breach of trust. But neither should authorize a state, regime, or armed movement claiming to enforce Islamic criminal law to whip or kill. The next chapter examines the related but distinct protection of reputation against sexual accusation.

Chapter Eight

Qadhf, Reputation, and Unequal Protection of Dignity

The law of qadhf addresses a real and serious human injury: the destruction of reputation through false sexual accusation. A person publicly accused of zinā may suffer humiliation, family conflict, social exclusion, marital breakdown, economic loss, and even physical danger. The Qur'anic response is therefore morally significant. Those who accuse protected women and fail to produce four witnesses are subjected to a stated punishment, their testimony is rejected, and they are described as morally transgressive. Bahnasi presents this doctrine as evidence of the seriousness with which Islamic law protects reputation and restrains reckless sexual allegation.[88]

That protective purpose deserves recognition. The difficulty lies in the structure built around it. Classical doctrine does not protect every human being equally. Full protection may depend upon sanity, age, freedom, Islam, chastity, and other inherited conditions of legal status. The doctrine also extends into disputed forms of indirect language, imposes eighty lashes, and divides jurists over victim demand, pardon, repentance, and restoration of testimonial capacity. The question is therefore not whether reputation should be protected. It plainly should. The question is why dignity should depend upon status classifications and why reputational injury should be answered by corporal punishment rather than correction, retraction, compensation, and proportionate law.

The Nature and Legitimate Purpose of Qadhf

Bahnasi defines qadhf principally as a sufficiently direct accusation of zinā or a denial of legitimate lineage. Calling a person an adulterer, alleging unlawful sexual intercourse, or challenging paternity may bring the accusation within the doctrine because sexual reputation,

88Qur'an 24:4–5. See also Aḥmad Fatḥī Bahnasi, Al-Ḥudūd fī al-Islām (Alexandria: Mu'assasat Shabāb al-Jāmi'a, n.d.), 99–139, on qadhf, its punishment, and its relation to reputation and testimony.

lineage, marriage, and family standing were closely connected in the classical social order.[89]

The moral objective remains entirely intelligible. False accusation, malicious publication, fabricated evidence, reputational harassment, and knowingly false reporting can cause grave and lasting harm. Modern law also protects reputation. The disagreement concerns the equality and method of protection. Speech may require legal accountability, but accountability should address the falsehood and its consequences rather than make the body of the speaker the principal object of punishment.

Explicit and Indirect Accusation

The clearest case is an explicit factual accusation. Bahnasi also considers conditional, future, written, and indirect statements. The doctrine must distinguish a completed allegation from prediction, quotation, hypothetical speech, insult, and ambiguous correspondence. These distinctions are understandable, but they demonstrate that liability depends upon linguistic interpretation rather than a self-applying rule.

The most disputed category is taʿrīḍ, insinuated accusation. Some jurists confine the fixed punishment to explicit words and leave insinuation to taʿzīr. Mālik and others permit the ḥadd where context and intention clearly communicate the accusation. A person may therefore receive eighty lashes under one interpretation and no ḥadd under another. Tone, sarcasm, anger, cultural idiom, and incomplete recollection make intention difficult to prove. Corporal punishment should not rest upon such uncertainty.[90]

Truth, Proof, and the Danger of Silencing Victims

Qadhf is tied closely to the extraordinary proof required for zinā. An accuser may sincerely believe that misconduct occurred and may even be factually correct, yet become liable if four qualified witnesses cannot

---

89Bahnasi, Al-Ḥudūd fī al-Islām, 99–139, on direct accusation of zinā, denial of lineage, and the legal elements of qadhf.

90Bahnasi, Al-Ḥudūd fī al-Islām, 99–139, on the four-witness requirement and the legal relationship between qadhf and accusations of zinā.

establish the act in the required manner. The rule protects people from rumor and reckless scandal, but it also creates a distinction between truth and legally demonstrable truth.

That distinction becomes dangerous when speech arises from rape, coercion, harassment, safeguarding, medical treatment, custody litigation, or confidential legal advice. A victim of sexual violence must never be treated as a qādhif merely because four eyewitnesses do not exist. Your dissertation identified this danger directly, noting that women may fear reporting rape because failure to satisfy the four-witness structure can expose them to accusations of qadhf or zinā.[91]

A modern system must distinguish malicious public accusation from good-faith reporting to competent authorities. It must use evidence appropriate to rape, abuse, coercion, and harassment rather than transfer the evidentiary structure of consensual zinā into sexual-violence cases.

Unequal Protection Through the Status of the Accused

Bahnasi's account makes the legal status of the accused person decisive. The protected person must satisfy conditions associated with iḥṣān for qadhf, including sanity, maturity according to disputed views, freedom, Islam, chastity, and identification. These are not merely procedural qualifications. They determine whether the accuser receives the full corporal punishment.[92]

A person with mental illness still possesses dignity and may be especially vulnerable to ridicule. A child falsely accused of sexual conduct may suffer devastating harm and should ordinarily receive stronger protection, not weaker protection. Yet classical disagreement over sanity and age filters the injury through legal capacity.

The distinction between free and enslaved persons is even more direct. The same accusation could generate different punishment depending upon the victim's status. Your dissertation records the

---

91Mark A. Gabriel, "Reforming Hudud Ordinances to Reconcile Islamic Criminal Law with International Human Rights Law" (PhD diss., University of Cape Town, 2016), 100–101, 124–25. The dissertation identifies the danger that rape victims and witnesses may fear qadhf liability where four eyewitnesses cannot be produced.

92Bahnasi, Al-Ḥudūd fī al-Islām, 99–139, on the conditions of the accuser, accused, wording, and protected status in qadhf.

classical differentiation between accusation of a free person and accusation of an enslaved person. The injury to dignity was therefore measured through hierarchy.[93]

Religion creates another inequality. Under the dominant position described by Bahnasi, accusation of a Muslim may receive full ḥadd protection while accusation of a Jewish or Christian person may receive lesser or discretionary protection. A false sexual allegation harms a human being regardless of religion. Equal citizenship cannot preserve a hierarchy in which Muslim dignity receives one legal value and non-Muslim dignity another.

Chastity also functions as a condition. A person previously associated with zinā may lose full protection against a later accusation. This converts past moral history into present eligibility for dignity. Even a person who previously sinned, repented, or acquired a damaged reputation remains entitled not to be subjected to new falsehood. Past misconduct does not cancel present personhood.

Victim Demand, Pardon, and Ownership of the Injury

Bahnasi records disagreement over whether qadhf requires a complaint by the injured person and whether pardon extinguishes punishment. One approach emphasizes the individual right; another gives greater weight to the right of God or public morality. The dispute concerns who owns the injury.[94]

Because the harm is reputational and deeply personal, the victim may prefer privacy, apology, retraction, compensation, removal of publication, or an end to proceedings. A trial can repeat the accusation and deepen humiliation. A system genuinely concerned with dignity should give substantial weight to the victim's wishes rather than allow public authority to seize the injury and continue flogging against the victim's preference.

93Bahnasi, Al-Ḥudūd fī al-Islām, 99–139, on the punishment for qadhf and the additional consequence for testimonial capacity.

94Bahnasi, Al-Ḥudūd fī al-Islām, 99–139, on disagreement over whether qadhf is predominantly a private right, a right of God, or a mixed right, and the resulting consequences for victim demand and pardon.

Proof, Judicial Knowledge, and Linguistic Uncertainty

Bahnasi explains that qadhf may be proven through testimony or confession and records disagreement over whether a judge may rely upon personal knowledge. The court must determine the exact words, context, identity of the target, whether the statement was quotation or assertion, and whether the witnesses heard the same accusation. Where punishment is corporal, small differences become highly consequential.

The more protective position separates witness and judge. A judge personally involved in the incident may become emotionally invested or may unconsciously defend personal credibility. The existence of disagreement again confirms that the procedural route to the ḥadd was humanly constructed rather than uniformly fixed.

Punishment, Testimonial Disqualification, and Repentance

Bahnasi identifies three principal consequences associated with the Qur'anic text: eighty lashes, rejection of the accuser's testimony, and classification of the accuser as morally transgressive. These consequences affect the body, legal credibility, and moral standing.[95]

Flogging does not repair the reputational injury. It does not retract the allegation, correct the public record, remove online publication, restore a marriage, or compensate economic loss. A person falsely accused ordinarily needs affirmative correction: declaration of falsity, public retraction, removal, apology, compensation, protection from repetition, and confidential legal remedies. Punishment and restoration are not the same.

Jurists also disagreed over whether repentance restores testimonial capacity. One position preserves disqualification even after repentance; another allows legal credibility to return. The disagreement concerns rehabilitation. A legal order informed by repentance should hesitate before imposing permanent civil degradation. Individualized assessment is more consistent with moral transformation than lifelong exclusion.[96]

95Bahnasi, Al-Ḥudūd fī al-Islām, 99–139, on victim demand, pardon, and the mixed public-private character of qadhf.

96Bahnasi, Al-Ḥudūd fī al-Islām, 99–139, recording disagreement over whether repentance restores testimonial capacity after conviction

Multiple Accusations and Liʿān

Classical doctrine also debates whether accusations against several people produce one punishment or several. Modern law can recognize multiple victims, aggravate sentence, or award separate damages without multiplying corporal punishment.

Bahnasi discusses liʿān, the special Qur'anic procedure for a husband who accuses his wife but lacks four witnesses. The procedure replaces ordinary qadhf liability with reciprocal solemn declarations and consequences for the marriage. Its historical rationale is understandable because marital intimacy makes four witnesses virtually impossible and paternity may be directly contested. Yet it gives the husband a special evidentiary pathway unavailable to an unrelated accuser and must be examined in light of marital power, jealousy, coercion, divorce conflict, and child welfare.[97]

The Protective Achievement and Its Central Contradiction

A fair assessment must acknowledge the doctrine's achievement. It sought to stop sexual rumor, protect family reputation, preserve lineage, discipline speech, and prevent unsupported accusations. It also restrained the machinery of zinā by making public accusation dangerous where proof was absent. In that sense, qadhf created a procedural shield around private life.

But the shield was distributed unequally. Full protection could depend upon freedom, Islam, sanity, maturity, chastity, and recognized status. The doctrine proclaims the importance of dignity while allocating dignity hierarchically. This contradiction cannot be corrected merely by improving procedure.

A Constructive Modern Alternative

A modern framework should protect every person against malicious false sexual accusation regardless of religion, sex, disability, prior sexual history, marital status, ancestry, or social position. It should

---

for qadhf.

97Qur'an 24:6–9; Bahnasi, Al-Ḥudūd fī al-Islām, 99–139, on liʿān as a special marital procedure replacing ordinary qadhf liability where a husband accuses his wife without four witnesses.

distinguish deliberate falsehood, reckless publication, good-faith reporting, privileged legal communication, journalism, medical disclosure, safeguarding, and testimony in court. Truth should ordinarily be a defense where lawfully relevant, and good-faith reporting to competent authorities must be protected.

Proportionality also matters. A private outburst differs from mass publication; an immediate retraction differs from a calculated campaign; a reasonable mistake differs from malicious fabrication. Law should consider audience, intention, repetition, actual harm, apology, retraction, and economic consequence. A fixed corporal punishment cannot reflect these differences adequately.

The legitimate purpose of qadhf can be preserved through civil defamation remedies, narrowly defined criminal liability for knowingly false and seriously harmful accusations, compensation, correction, removal orders, confidentiality, and penalties for retaliation against legitimate complainants. Religious communities may continue to teach truthfulness, restraint, concealment of private wrongdoing, repentance, apology, reconciliation, and protection of the vulnerable. Those moral teachings do not require flogging.[98]

98Gabriel, "Reforming Hudud Ordinances," 191–92, proposing replacement of flogging for qadhf with penalties capable of protecting reputation without corporal punishment; see also 198–99 on individualized taʿzīr and human-rights-compatible alternatives.

Conclusion

Bahnasi's treatment of qadhf demonstrates one of the strongest moral concerns within the ḥudūd tradition: human reputation must not be destroyed by unsupported sexual allegation. The doctrine carefully examines language, intention, victim identity, proof, demand, pardon, liʿān, testimonial exclusion, and repentance. This complexity shows sustained juristic concern. It also shows that the offense is constructed through disputed judgments about speech, status, and the relationship between public and private rights.

The tension is direct:

> *The doctrine protects reputation powerfully, but not universally; it punishes false accusation severely, but not restoratively.*

Every human being possesses reputation and dignity. Protection against sexual defamation should not depend upon religion, freedom, prior chastity, sanity, or inherited status, and it should not require a state, regime, or armed movement claiming to enforce Islamic criminal law to flog the speaker. The law should repair falsehood through truth, retraction, compensation, correction, and proportionate accountability. Dignity is best protected when it is treated as universal. The next chapter examines alcohol, intoxication, and the difference between religious prohibition and criminal punishment.

Chapter Nine

Alcohol, Intoxication, and the Difference Between Prohibition and Criminal Punishment

The Islamic prohibition of intoxicants presents a different problem from theft, ḥirāba, zinā, and qadhf. The Qur'anic moral judgment is strong and unmistakable. Intoxicants are associated with harm, hostility, interference with prayer, and impairment of reason, and believers are instructed to avoid them. The principal question is therefore not whether Islam prohibits intoxicating drink. It is whether that religious prohibition also establishes one clear, fixed, and universally applicable corporal punishment for consumption.[99]

Aḥmad Fatḥī Bahnasi's treatment demonstrates that these are separate questions. The prohibition is presented with confidence, but the criminal definition and punishment depend upon disagreement over the meaning of khamr, the substance from which a drink is made, the amount consumed, whether actual intoxication occurred, knowledge, coercion, necessity, proof, and the number and legal character of the lashes. The central argument of this chapter is therefore:

> *A clear moral prohibition does not automatically produce a clear criminal offense, and a criminal prohibition does not automatically establish one divinely fixed punishment.*

The Gradual Qur'anic Prohibition

Bahnasi explains the prohibition through the familiar Qur'anic progression. Intoxicants and gambling are first described as containing both benefit and grave sin, with the sin greater than the benefit. Believers are then forbidden to approach prayer while intoxicated. Finally, intoxicants, gambling, idols, and divining practices are described as defilement from the work of Satan, and believers are

99Qur'an 2:219; 4:43; 5:90–91. See also Aḥmad Fatḥī Bahnasi, Al-Ḥudūd fī al-Islām (Alexandria: Mu'assasat Shabāb al-Jāmiʿa, n.d.), 145 –59.

commanded to avoid them. The text associates intoxicants with hostility, hatred, distraction from remembrance of God, and interference with prayer.[100]

This gradual development has moral and historical importance. It reflects education, persuasion, and social transformation before final prohibition. It does not, however, state forty lashes, eighty lashes, a particular instrument, or any numerically fixed corporal sentence. Religious prohibition belongs to the moral command; state punishment requires an additional legal construction.

The Meaning of Khamr

Bahnasi presents disagreement over the legal meaning of khamr. Mālik, al-Shāfiʿī, Aḥmad, and associated jurists generally adopt a broad definition: every intoxicating beverage is prohibited, regardless of whether it is made from grapes, dates, honey, grain, or another substance. The position associated with Iraqi and Ḥanafī jurists distinguishes more carefully between grape wine and other fermented drinks, sometimes making liability for the latter depend upon actual intoxication or particular conditions.[101]

The disagreement is not necessarily about whether intoxication is morally acceptable. It concerns legal classification. Does khamr name grape wine specifically, every fermented drink, every intoxicating beverage, or every substance that obscures the intellect? The answer affects whether a small amount is punishable, whether actual intoxication must occur, whether the fixed punishment applies, and which evidentiary rules govern. A modern government cannot move directly from the general Qur'anic condemnation to one unified criminal code. It must first select a juristic theory.

100Bahnasi, Al-Ḥudūd fī al-Islām, 145–49, on the gradual Qur'anic prohibition and the movement from acknowledgment of harm to abstention.

101Bahnasi, Al-Ḥudūd fī al-Islām, 145–53, recording disagreement over the linguistic and legal meaning of khamr and the treatment of intoxicants made from substances other than grapes.

Consumption, Intoxication, and Modern Substances

The difference between substance-based and effect-based liability is substantial. Under one model, any quantity of a beverage whose large quantity intoxicates is prohibited. Under another, the decisive issue may be whether intoxication actually occurred. A small amount may affect people differently because of body weight, health, medication, or tolerance. Food, medicine, and manufactured products may contain trace alcohol. Modern intoxicants may include narcotics, synthetic drugs, inhalants, pharmaceuticals, and chemical substances unknown to the classical jurists.[102]

A coherent modern law must decide whether it punishes the substance, the amount, intention, impairment, or harmful conduct resulting from impairment. Extending a classical beverage category to modern drugs requires analogy, scientific classification, and legislation. The contemporary authority is therefore constructing a new regulatory framework, not merely restoring a complete revealed code.

Knowledge, Coercion, and Necessity

Criminal responsibility requires knowledge and voluntariness. A person may consume a mislabeled drink, unknowingly ingest alcohol in food or medicine, or misunderstand the nature of a substance. Bahnasi also examines coercion, distinguishing cases where meaningful choice is removed from those in which some capacity to resist is thought to remain. The principle is sound, but the line between complete and incomplete coercion depends upon delicate factual judgments about threats, immediacy, fear, escape, physical force, and danger to family members.[103]

Necessity further demonstrates that the same physical act does not carry one moral meaning independent of context. Bahnasi discusses severe thirst, choking, hunger, and threats to life. Modern questions

---

102Bahnasi, Al-Ḥudūd fī al-Islām, 145–53, on small and large quantities, actual intoxication, and substances treated by analogy. See also Mohammad Hashim Kamali, Shariah Law: An Introduction (Oxford: Oneworld, 2008), 199–204.

103Bahnasi, Al-Ḥudūd fī al-Islām, 145–59, on proof of drinking or intoxication by confession, testimony, and disputed evidentiary indications.

extend to medicines containing alcohol, emergency treatment, therapeutic use, food preparation, and trace quantities. Such issues require current medical evidence concerning physiology, toxicity, concentration, and available alternatives. A contemporary government cannot responsibly codify premodern factual assumptions without scientific review.

The Number of Lashes

The Qur'an prohibits intoxicants but does not assign a stated number of lashes. The numerical punishment arises from reports of prophetic and early caliphal practice. Those reports describe striking with hands, sandals, garments, palm branches, and other available means. The practice was not initially presented as one precisely measured sentence administered through a uniform instrument.[104]

Reports associated with the Prophet and Abū Bakr are commonly understood as supporting approximately forty lashes. Under ʿUmar, the number was increased to eighty after consultation. Bahnasi presents the reasoning attributed to ʿAlī: a drinker may become intoxicated; the intoxicated person may speak irrationally; irrational speech may lead to false accusation; and qadhf carries eighty lashes. This is analogy and governmental policy, not a direct numerical command of revelation.[105]

The reasoning also punishes a possible consequence rather than an offense actually committed. Many persons who drink do not falsely accuse anyone of zinā. A person should be punished for slander actually committed, not for the possibility that intoxication could lead to it.

Jurists consequently differed over whether forty is the fixed ḥadd and the additional forty a discretionary taʿzīr, whether eighty became the established punishment through caliphal policy, or whether the ruler retains flexibility. Variation in instrument, number, analogy, and governmental adjustment points more naturally toward taʿzīr than toward one immutable corporal sentence.

104Bahnasi, Al-Ḥudūd fī al-Islām, 145–59, recording the absence of a Qur'anic numerical punishment for drinking and the development of forty- and eighty-lash positions in later practice.

105Bahnasi, Al-Ḥudūd fī al-Islām, 145–59, on the reported use of hands, garments, sandals, and palm branches before later numerical standardization.

Private Sin and Public Harm

A religious community may teach complete abstinence, and a Muslim may abstain because of faith, conscience, health, or family responsibility. A plural modern state must nevertheless distinguish private consumption from public disorder, impaired driving, violence, workplace danger, supplying minors, child neglect, and other demonstrable harms. These situations do not carry the same legal character.

The state has strong grounds to punish conduct that endangers others: driving while impaired, operating dangerous machinery, assault, neglect, unlawful distribution, and public disorder. It does not need to enter a private home merely to discover whether a competent adult consumed a religiously prohibited beverage. Private consumption may remain sinful without becoming a corporal crime.

Addiction, Public Health, and Rational Regulation

Alcohol dependence raises questions that flogging cannot answer. A person may remain responsible for violence, dangerous driving, or neglect, but repeated bodily punishment may deepen shame, increase secrecy, discourage treatment, and fail to prevent relapse. A rational response should include treatment, medical care, counseling, rehabilitation, and family support while preserving accountability for concrete harm.[106]

Alcohol misuse is also a matter of public health, traffic safety, family welfare, workplace regulation, and commercial licensing. Age restrictions, licensing, taxation, warning labels, advertising controls, impaired-driving laws, treatment programs, and targeted penalties are more precise than a universal corporal sentence. A legal system justified by preservation of reason should use methods capable of addressing impaired judgment and dependency rather than merely striking the body.

106Bahnasi, Al-Ḥudūd fī al-Islām, 154–59, on the argument attributed to ʿAlī connecting intoxication, irrational speech, qadhf, and eighty lashes.

Equality, Religious Identity, and Selective Enforcement

A state containing Muslims, Christians, Jews, adherents of other religions, and persons without religious affiliation faces an unavoidable equality problem. If the offense applies only to Muslims, criminal responsibility depends upon religion. If it applies to everyone, non-Muslims are compelled to observe one religion's dietary rule. A religion-specific offense would also require the government to determine who is legally Muslim, including converts, persons who no longer believe, mixed families, visitors, and disputed identities.[107]

Morality offenses are also vulnerable to selective enforcement. The poor, young people, women, minorities, dissidents, and socially visible offenders may be prosecuted, while wealthier citizens drink privately and remain unseen. Police may use allegations of drinking as a pretext for searches, detention, or pressure. A formally religious law may therefore produce deeply unequal practice.

Proof, Surveillance, and State Responsibility

A modern prosecution would need to prove the substance, chemical composition, quantity, knowledge, voluntariness, and absence of lawful exception. Evidence might include confession, testimony, smell, behavior, possession, breath testing, blood analysis, or video. Each method requires safeguards: smell may be mistaken, illness may resemble intoxication, possession does not prove consumption, laboratory evidence requires chain of custody, and confession may be coerced.

The government would therefore have to build a complete forensic and procedural code around a punishment that the Qur'an never numerically stated. Enforcement may also encourage surveillance of homes, gatherings, hotels, restaurants, vehicles, and personal belongings. A command addressed to conscience becomes a mandate for police intrusion.

107Bahnasi, Al-Ḥudūd fī al-Islām, 145–59, on the juristic construction of punishment for intoxicants; Gabriel, "Reforming Hudud Ordinances," discussion of alcohol and alternative sanctions.

Deterrence and the Body

Defenders of corporal punishment may argue that flogging deters consumption and protects society. But deterrence cannot be assumed from severity. The relevant questions are whether flogging reduces harmful drinking, addiction, violence, and accidents; whether it merely drives conduct underground; whether it discourages medical treatment; and whether targeted safety laws and treatment would work better.

Flogging turns the body into the site upon which government expresses moral condemnation. The pain is intended to punish, discipline, deter, and communicate seriousness. Yet the body is not the source of addiction, social pressure, poor judgment, or emotional distress. Striking it does not necessarily restore reason.

A Constructive Alternative

The legitimate moral concerns associated with the prohibition can be preserved without flogging. A modern framework may punish impaired driving and violent conduct, regulate dangerous sale and distribution, protect minors, require workplace sobriety in hazardous occupations, intervene in neglect, provide addiction treatment, support families, educate the public, and permit religious communities to teach abstinence openly and seriously.

Gabriel's earlier doctoral research concluded that the Qur'an assigns no corporal punishment for drinking, that the schools disagree substantially over definition, proof, number, and method, and that the sentence cannot properly be described as divine and infallible. It proposed treating the matter, where public law requires regulation, through proportionate taʿzīr rather than a fixed ḥadd. The present book advances that conclusion by separating private religious abstinence from state punishment and directing criminal law toward concrete harm.[108]

108Bahnasi, Al-Ḥudūd fī al-Islām, 145–59, recording disagreement over the meaning of khamr, the scope of intoxicants, proof, and punishment.

Conclusion

Bahnasi's discussion begins from an undisputed religious foundation: intoxicants are prohibited in Islam. He presents the gradual Qur'anic movement toward abstention and the moral concern for reason, prayer, family, and social order. But the penal structure is not equally clear. The schools dispute the meaning of khamr, the treatment of different substances, small and large quantities, consumption and intoxication, coercion, necessity, proof, the number of lashes, and whether the punishment is fixed or discretionary.

The textual point is decisive:

> *The Qur'anic prohibition of intoxicants does not itself establish one numerically explicit, universally defined, state-administered corporal punishment.*

A modern government that chooses forty or eighty lashes has selected a definition, evidentiary structure, set of exceptions, and number of strokes. It cannot make those human choices and then deny responsibility for them. Society may regulate intoxication firmly, protect others from danger, support abstinence, and treat addiction. But no state, regime, or armed movement claiming to enforce Islamic criminal law should convert a moral command addressed to conscience into an automatic mandate for flogging. The next chapter examines how procedural doctrines repeatedly function as an escape from substantive severity.

Chapter Ten

Procedure as an Escape from Substantive Severity

One of the most striking features of Bahnasi's presentation is the contrast between the severity of the substantive punishments and the caution of the procedural doctrines surrounding them. The substantive law authorizes amputation, cross-amputation, flogging, stoning, crucifixion, exile, and execution. The procedural law, however, repeatedly creates reasons to prevent those punishments from being reached. Bahnasi discusses legal doubt, demanding witness requirements, strict agreement among witnesses, reluctance to accept confession, retraction, concealment, necessity, coercion, uncertain ownership, repentance before capture, limits upon judicial knowledge, and disputes over whether a victim's demand is required.[109]

These doctrines are often presented as evidence that Islamic criminal law combines severity with mercy. That description contains an important truth. Classical jurists recognized the danger of wrongful and excessive punishment and developed safeguards that often made enforcement difficult. Yet those safeguards also reveal a deeper structural problem:

> *Procedure becomes the principal location of mercy because the substantive punishment has been placed beyond ordinary reconsideration.*

The Doctrine of Doubt

The most important general principle is the instruction to avert the ḥudūd in cases of legally significant doubt. Bahnasi invokes this principle throughout his treatment. Doubt may concern ownership, marriage, consent, coercion, necessity, identity, legal capacity, the meaning of words, the substance consumed, the status of the accused,

---

109 Aḥmad Fatḥī Bahnasi, Al-Ḥudūd fī al-Islām (Alexandria: Mu'assasat Shabāb al-Jāmi'a, n.d.), 61–90, 99–159, together with his sections on ḥirāba and zinā. For a comparative account of the school disagreements across these offenses, see Gabriel, "Reforming Hudud Ordinances," 93–126.

confession, or interpretation of evidence. The doctrine is one of the strongest expressions of caution within the classical tradition.[110]

Yet doubt is itself a juristic category. Courts must decide what kind of uncertainty counts, how strong it must be, whether it concerns facts or law, whether the accused sincerely believed in the claimed entitlement, and whether the governing school recognizes the alleged ambiguity. One jurist may see a doubt where another does not. The protection is therefore substantial but not uniform.

The doctrine becomes necessary because the punishment is treated as fixed once liability is established. The structure operates through thresholds: either the offense is established and the ḥadd follows, or a recognized doubt prevents the ḥadd and some other liability may remain. A small difference in classification can separate amputation from taʿzīr, stoning from no ḥadd, or flogging from removal of the fixed category. Procedure carries the burden that proportional sentencing would otherwise bear.

Confession, Reluctance, and Retraction

Confession occupies a central place because several ḥadd offenses are difficult to prove through witnesses. In the zinā reports presented by Bahnasi, the authority does not appear eager to receive a confession and proceed immediately to punishment. The confessor is questioned, turned away, examined for sanity, and given opportunities to reconsider. Jurists then disagree over whether one admission is sufficient or whether four separate confessions are required.[111]

This reluctance reflects a morally significant principle: the state should not rush to convert private sin into public punishment. But it also raises a difficult question. Why retain a punishment that becomes

---

110 Bahnasi, Al-Ḥudūd fī al-Islām, discussions of shubha and avoidance of the ḥudūd; see also Gabriel, "Reforming Hudud Ordinances," 98–100, 160–97, on doubt, evidentiary restrictions, necessity, and reform.

111 Bahnasi, Al-Ḥudūd fī al-Islām, section on zinā, on confession, repeated admission, inquiry into capacity, and reluctance to proceed rapidly to punishment; Gabriel, "Reforming Hudud Ordinances," 98–100.

reachable largely when a person persists in confessing despite efforts to turn him or her away?

A confession may arise from sincere repentance, but also from depression, shame, family coercion, fear of divine punishment, manipulation, psychological distress, or a desire for death. Legal competence does not guarantee psychological freedom. Where the consequence is flogging, amputation, or death, ordinary voluntariness standards are not sufficient.

Bahnasi also records disagreement over retraction. Some jurists permit withdrawal because it creates doubt; others hold that a valid confession may continue to establish liability. The disagreement becomes especially grave where punishment has begun and the accused attempts to flee or disavow the admission. For irreversible punishment, retraction should require immediate suspension and complete review.[112]

Witness Testimony and Evidentiary Barriers

The four-witness requirement for zinā is among the most demanding rules in the classical penal system. Witnesses must be legally qualified, directly observe the act, agree concerning its essential circumstances, and avoid material contradiction. The rule protects against rumor, suspicion, ordinary observation of intimacy, and reputational accusation. It also makes conviction nearly impossible where the conduct remains private.[113]

The strict proof requirement is often used to defend stoning or flogging: the punishment is said to be just because conviction is rare. But rarity of enforcement does not establish proportionality. It establishes that the legal system is reluctant to reach the punishment. A severe law does not become humane merely because procedure usually prevents its use.

Witness qualification raises a further difficulty. Requirements of adulthood, sanity, moral reliability, direct observation, and agreement

---

112 Bahnasi, Al-Ḥudūd fī al-Islām, section on zinā, recording disagreement over retraction of confession and its legal effect; Gabriel, "Reforming Hudud Ordinances," 98–100, 188–90.

113 Qur'an 24:4; Bahnasi, Al-Ḥudūd fī al-Islām, section on zinā, on four eyewitnesses, direct observation, agreement, and witness qualification; Gabriel, "Reforming Hudud Ordinances," 98–100.

seek to protect the accused. Yet classical rules of testimonial competence may also reflect unequal classifications based upon sex, religion, freedom, or social status. Procedure cannot be called just merely because it is strict; it must also be equal.

Witnesses who fail to complete the required proof may themselves risk qadhf liability. This can restrain reckless accusation and protect privacy. It can also discourage legitimate reporting where a person cannot guarantee that three additional witnesses will testify consistently. The threat of corporal punishment regulates not only falsehood but also the willingness to report.

Judicial Knowledge, Delay, and Institutional Separation

Bahnasi discusses whether a judge may impose a ḥadd on the basis of personal knowledge. The safer position requires formal proof rather than allowing the judge to become both witness and adjudicator. That separation is sound. A judge who personally observed or experienced the event may be emotionally involved and unable to maintain the distance required for adjudication.[114]

He also records disagreement over delayed testimony. Some jurists treat unexplained delay as suspicious; others recognize that fear, absence, uncertainty, or another legitimate impediment may justify it. The court must evaluate memory, motive, pressure, and circumstance. These are ordinary problems of evidence, but they become extraordinary where the sentence may be death or mutilation.

Concealment and the Contradiction of Public Punishment

Bahnasi presents concealment of private wrongdoing as a major moral principle, especially in sexual offenses. A person should not rush to expose another's private sin, and repentance may occur without prosecution. This principle reflects a restrained view of state authority and provides one of the strongest arguments for removing consensual private morality from criminal enforcement.[115]

---

114 Bahnasi, Al-Ḥudūd fī al-Islām, discussions of the judge's personal knowledge and delayed testimony in zinā and qadhf. For the wider evidentiary framework and its disagreements, see Gabriel, "Reforming Hudud Ordinances," 98–101, 124–26.

The same system that favors concealment may later demand public flogging or stoning once proof is complete. Before proof, privacy is protected; after proof, the body becomes public spectacle. Strict evidence does not resolve the contradiction. The question remains why the state should convert private immorality into public bodily punishment at all.

Necessity, Coercion, and Social Responsibility

Necessity appears in theft and drinking. A starving person who takes food does not stand in the same moral position as a professional thief, and a person who consumes a prohibited substance to preserve life does not act with ordinary criminal intent. The principle is humane because it recognizes that context determines culpability.[116]

The famine example associated with ʿUmar raises an additional question of state responsibility. Before punishing theft, government must ask whether it provided food security, access to assistance, economic justice, and meaningful alternatives to survival crime. An authority that fails in those obligations should not mutilate the person suffering from the consequences of that failure.

Coercion also exists along a spectrum, including direct violence, threats, family domination, economic dependence, institutional pressure, and fear of serious loss. The classical distinction between complete and incomplete coercion attempts to draw a line, but modern experience confirms that the line is often uncertain. Bodily and irreversible punishment should not be imposed on the basis of an uncertain conclusion that the accused could have resisted.

Ownership Doubt and Protected Custody

The law of theft provides clear examples of procedural escape. Doubt may arise from debt, family relationship, common ownership, public

---

115 Bahnasi, Al-Ḥudūd fī al-Islām, section on zinā, emphasizing concealment of private wrongdoing and restraint in enforcement. See also Gabriel, "Reforming Hudud Ordinances," 98–100, 188–90, on the exceptionally demanding proof structure.

116Bahnasi, Al-Ḥudūd fī al-Islām, chapters on theft and drinking, on necessity, famine, coercion, and emergency circumstances; Gabriel, "Reforming Hudud Ordinances," 193–94.

treasury interests, marital access, employment, or another claim of entitlement. Where the doubt is legally recognized, amputation falls even if wrongful taking occurred. The doctrine protects against extreme punishment where ownership relations are ambiguous, but it also proves that the state must resolve complex civil questions before it can claim to administer a fixed divine sentence.[117]

The requirement of ḥirz adds a customary judgment. Whether property was adequately protected depends upon place, object, social practice, technology, and authorized access. A difference in customary evaluation may determine whether the accused loses a hand. The procedural protection is real; the underlying punishment remains disproportionate to the uncertainty of the classification.

Victim Demand, Referral, and the Point Where Mercy Narrows

Bahnasi records circumstances in which the victim's complaint or demand matters even where an offense is classified partly as a right of God. In theft, the owner may possess information concerning permission, debt, or ownership. In qadhf, jurists disagree over whether the injured person must demand enforcement because the offense contains personal and public dimensions. These rules reveal that the distinction between divine and individual rights is unstable in practice.[118]

A recurring classical distinction separates the period before referral to public authority from the period after formal referral and completion of proof. Before referral, pardon, settlement, concealment, or private resolution may remain possible. After the case reaches the ruler, intercession narrows sharply. The same act may be forgivable before official involvement and mandatory afterward.

This means that the state's entry may reduce mercy rather than enlarge justice. The victim may forgive, the offender may repent, and

---

117Bahnasi, Al-Ḥudūd fī al-Islām, 61–90, on debt, shared ownership, family relationships, public funds, employment access, and ḥirz.

118Bahnasi, Al-Ḥudūd fī al-Islām, 61–90 (theft) and 99–139 (qadhf), on victim demand, pardon, referral to authority, and the mixed character of private and public rights.

the harm may be repaired, yet government may claim that the case is no longer subject to human control. This is sacralized coercion in procedural form.

Repentance, Timing, and Technical Failure

In ḥirāba, repentance before capture may remove the public ḥadd while victims' rights remain. The rule encourages surrender and cessation of violence. But it creates a rigid temporal boundary: repentance before capture has major legal effect, while the same moral transformation after capture may not. What changes is the state's possession of the accused.[119]

Timing matters throughout the system: confession before or after retraction, pardon before or after referral, repentance before or after capture, testimony given promptly or after delay, and ownership claimed before or after prosecution. Such distinctions may be administratively necessary, but they become morally troubling when they determine life, limb, or bodily integrity.

The procedural system often works through technical exclusion. A case fails because one witness is missing, the words were indirect, ownership was doubtful, a confession was withdrawn, the marriage was defective, the accused lacked a status requirement, or testimony was delayed. This may save the accused without establishing innocence. The person may still face taʿzīr, stigma, exposure, or another form of coercion.

The Danger of Evidentiary Substitution

Acquittal from the ḥadd is not always acquittal from state punishment. Where strict proof fails, Bahnasi often leaves discretionary punishment available. This may be more humane, but it also creates a danger: taʿzīr may become a means to punish an accused person for an offense the state could not prove under the governing evidentiary standard.

If circumstantial evidence insufficient for zinā nevertheless produces severe discretionary punishment, or if failure to establish ḥirz is followed by a sentence resembling the avoided ḥadd, the safeguard

---

119 Qur'an 5:34; Bahnasi, Al-Ḥudūd fī al-Islām, section on ḥirāba, on repentance before capture and survival of victims' private claims; Gabriel, "Reforming Hudud Ordinances," 196–99.

becomes illusory. A constitutional system must prevent discretionary punishment from reproducing the fixed penalty through another label.

Procedure Cannot Cure Substantive Injustice

The strongest defense of the ḥudūd often rests upon procedure: proof is difficult, doubt prevents punishment, confession may be withdrawn, private wrongdoing should be concealed, and judges should avoid enforcement where uncertainty exists. These safeguards reduce the number of cases. They do not answer the justice of the punishment once a case crosses the threshold.

Procedural safeguards address identification, voluntariness, evidence, defenses, and regularity. They do not determine whether the conduct should be criminalized, whether the sentence is proportionate, whether the law is equal, whether government possesses legitimate authority, or whether the punishment is compatible with dignity. A perfectly fair trial can still enforce an unjust law.

Bahnasi's work demonstrates genuine procedural sophistication. The jurists understood that witnesses fail, confessions may be unreliable, ownership is complex, coercion exists, necessity changes culpability, and state punishment can be dangerous. Their response was to surround severe penalties with caution. But the more elaborate the protections become, the more clearly they reveal fear of the punishment they surround.

Mercy Should Not Depend upon Technicality

A humane legal system should not require a judge to find an artificial defect in order to avoid an unjust result. Mercy should be available openly through proportionality, mitigation, pardon, rehabilitation, restorative justice, and legislative revision. Where compassion must hide inside technical doubt, substantive law has become too rigid.

The Modern State Magnifies the Risk

The classical evidentiary system developed without digital surveillance, DNA testing, electronic communication, forensic laboratories, biometric records, widespread cameras, and centralized police databases. A technologically powerful state may prove private conduct more easily than classical jurists imagined. Rules formed in a low-surveillance environment may produce far more convictions after transplantation into a modern security apparatus.[120]

Modern government must choose whether video, digital images, messages, forensic evidence, and location records satisfy or supplement classical proof. If it expands evidence, the traditional privacy barrier collapses. If it refuses modern evidence, the law becomes selectively archaic. Either choice requires modern legislation.

Modern interrogation also introduces detention, isolation, plea bargaining, family pressure, and abusive methods. A classical rule accepting confession cannot be transferred without strong protections against coercion. The danger is greatest in ḥirāba, rebellion, and apostasy, where government may regard the accused as a threat to its political or religious authority and ordinary safeguards may weaken.

A Constructive Modern Alternative

The classical procedural tradition contains principles worth preserving: punishment should be restrained; doubt should favor the accused; confession should be treated cautiously; coercion and necessity matter; private wrongdoing should not be exposed recklessly; judges should not combine incompatible roles; and surrender and repentance should be encouraged.

Those principles should be separated from the punishments they once surrounded. A modern system can embody caution through presumption of innocence, proof beyond reasonable doubt, exclusion of coerced confession, appellate review, individualized sentencing, proportionality, restorative justice, and compensation for wrongful conviction. Mercy then becomes part of the legal structure rather than an exception hidden inside technical failure.

120For the contrast between classical juristic procedure and modern centralized state enforcement, see Wael B. Hallaq, Shariʿa: Theory, Practice, Transformations (Cambridge: Cambridge University Press, 2009), 357–443.

Conclusion

Bahnasi's account does not describe a crude system eager to punish. It describes a system deeply concerned with avoiding error. That concern should be acknowledged honestly. But procedural caution does not vindicate amputation, stoning, crucifixion, or flogging. It reveals their danger.

The relationship can be stated simply:

> *The classical law preserves the severity of the ḥudūd by making their proof difficult, while the modern constitutional alternative should preserve the caution and abandon the severity.*

The system's mercy appears mainly at the gate. Once the gate is crossed, the punishment remains severe, irreversible, and frequently disproportionate. A modern legal order should not depend upon procedural escape from substantive injustice. It should make justice substantive. The next chapter examines the unequal legal personhood of those protected, accused, and heard within the classical penal order.

Chapter Eleven

Unequal Legal Personhood in the Classical Penal Order

The classical penal law described by Aḥmad Fatḥī Bahnasi does not operate upon one uniform legal person. Its rules developed within a social order that distinguished people according to religion, freedom, sex, marital history, chastity, age, sanity, residence, and testimonial capacity. These distinctions affected who received full protection, whose accusation triggered a fixed punishment, whose testimony was accepted, whether an accused person qualified for flogging or stoning, and whether the same conduct carried the same legal consequence.[121]

The jurists did not necessarily regard these classifications as arbitrary. They belonged to the legal and social structure of their age. Freedom and slavery, Muslim and protected non-Muslim status, male and female roles, marriage, lineage, and moral reputation all carried consequences throughout the wider legal system. Historical explanation, however, is not contemporary justification. A modern constitutional order begins from a different principle:

> *Every human being possesses equal legal personhood, and criminal protection and responsibility should not depend upon inherited status.*

This chapter does not argue that classical jurists lacked concern for justice. It argues that the justice they pursued was organized through a stratified legal order that cannot be transferred into a modern state without reproducing inequality.

---

121 Aḥmad Fatḥī Bahnasi, Al-Ḥudūd fī al-Islām, Shuʿāʿ al-Islām no. 12 (Alexandria: Muʾassasat Shabāb al-Jāmiʿa, n.d.), discussions of status, testimony, iḥṣān, qadhf, zinā, ḥirāba, and drinking. See also Gabriel, "Reforming Hudud Ordinances," 95–100, 124–26, on status- and testimony-based distinctions.

Legal Personhood and Status

Legal personhood is more than biological humanity. It includes the capacity to receive equal protection, testify, bring a claim, possess rights independently, be believed, and receive the same basic legal treatment for the same conduct. Bahnasi's account repeatedly asks not only what happened, but who acted, against whom, and with what legal status. The answer may alter protection, proof, and punishment.

Freedom, Slavery, and Graded Bodies

The clearest historical distinction is between free and enslaved persons. Bahnasi records doctrines under which an enslaved person receives half the divisible corporal punishment imposed upon a free person, together with further disagreements concerning slavery in theft, ḥirāba, zinā, and qadhf. The reduction may appear as mitigation, but its premise is unequal legal value: the free and enslaved body are measured differently.[122]

The inequality is especially visible in qadhf. Under the dominant position recorded by Bahnasi, falsely accusing an enslaved person does not trigger the same full fixed punishment as accusing a free protected person. The same defamatory statement therefore receives a different legal response according to the victim's status. The doctrine protects reputation, but it does not treat dignity as universal.

Slavery also shaped the law of property. An enslaved person was treated as a responsible human actor while simultaneously existing within another person's ownership and household authority. Questions of maintenance, access, taking from a master, and possession were therefore structured by an institution modern law has rejected entirely. The classical rules cannot simply be detached from that legal world and transferred unchanged.

122Bahnasi, Al-Ḥudūd fī al-Islām, on the differentiated punishment and protection of free and enslaved persons. See also Mark A. Gabriel, "Reforming Hudud Ordinances to Reconcile Islamic Criminal Law with International Human Rights Law" (PhD diss., University of Cape Town, 2016), 99–100, 124–26.

Religion and Unequal Protection

Bahnasi's account also reflects distinctions between Muslims and non-Muslims in protection against qadhf, testimonial status, conditions of iḥṣān, alcohol regulation, and political membership. Under the dominant rule he records, the full fixed punishment for sexual defamation may depend upon the victim being Muslim. A false accusation against a Jewish or Christian person remains wrongful, but does not necessarily receive the same sanction.[123]

The human injury is the same kind of injury. A false sexual accusation can destroy the reputation of a Muslim, Christian, Jew, adherent of another religion, or person without religious affiliation. Equal citizenship cannot declare that one person's dignity is protected through a fixed divine punishment while another receives lesser or merely discretionary protection.

The alcohol offense creates the opposite difficulty. If criminal punishment applies only to Muslims, citizens committing the same physical act are treated differently according to faith. If it applies to everyone, non-Muslims are compelled to obey one religion's dietary rule. A religion-specific penal law also requires the state to determine who is legally Muslim, including converts, persons born into Muslim families who no longer believe, mixed families, disputed conversions, and persons refusing religious classification.

Islam is also disputed as a condition of iḥṣān for stoning. Some jurists require it; others focus upon valid marriage and consummation. The choice may determine whether a non-Muslim accused of zinā is flogged or killed. Before imposing death, the modern authority would have to select one theology of legal status.[124]

Sex, Testimony, and Unequal Visibility

The position of women within the evidentiary system presents another central problem. In the classical proof of zinā, the four witnesses are

---

123Bahnasi, Al-Ḥudūd fī al-Islām, 99–139, on Islam and freedom as conditions of full protection in qadhf; Gabriel, "Reforming Hudud Ordinances," 99–100, 124–26.

124 Bahnasi, Al-Ḥudūd fī al-Islām, section on zinā, on disputed conditions of iḥṣān, including Islam, valid marriage, and consummation; Gabriel, "Reforming Hudud Ordinances," 95–97.

traditionally understood as legally qualified men. A woman may observe relevant conduct, possess reliable knowledge, or be directly affected, yet not possess the same testimonial capacity for the fixed offense. Modern evidence law cannot presume that credibility follows sex. It must evaluate perception, consistency, corroboration, honesty, and reliability.[125]

Exclusion may sometimes be defended as protection from participation in severe punishment or from liability where accusation fails. But protection through exclusion remains disempowerment. Witnesses should be protected through fair procedure, not denied legal voice because of sex.

Pregnancy also creates unequal visibility. Bahnasi records disagreement over whether unexplained pregnancy in an unmarried woman may establish or support zinā, particularly in Mālikī reasoning, while other jurists recognize coercion, mistaken intercourse, or another doubt. The woman's body visibly records pregnancy; the male participant may remain hidden. A formally gender-neutral prohibition can therefore produce unequal enforcement.[126]

Pregnancy must never be treated as proof of consent. A legal system organized around unlawful intercourse rather than consent may force a rape victim to disprove zinā before she receives protection. Modern law must state clearly that rape is violence, that four eyewitnesses are not required to establish it, and that pregnancy cannot convert a possible victim into an accused person.

Bahnasi also records disagreement over women's liability in ḥirāba. Conduct-based responsibility is preferable to assumptions about gender roles. A woman who participates in armed violence should be judged according to individual conduct and culpability, not presumed incapable of the offense or held responsible merely through membership in a group.

---

125 Bahnasi, Al-Ḥudūd fī al-Islām, discussions of testimony in zinā and related witness qualifications; Gabriel, "Reforming Hudud Ordinances," 98–100, 124–26.

126 Bahnasi, Al-Ḥudūd fī al-Islām, section on zinā, on pregnancy as disputed evidence and the role of shubha; Gabriel, "Reforming Hudud Ordinances," 98–100, 124–26, 188–90.

Formal Equality and Social Conditions

Even where the same words apply to men and women, enforcement may not be equal. Women may face greater family surveillance, economic dependence, forced confession, reputational pressure, restricted mobility, and weaker access to counsel. Equal wording is not enough. A constitutional system must examine the actual distribution of vulnerability and state power.

Marital History and the Status of Iḥṣān

The division between muḥṣan and non-muḥṣan creates another form of unequal legal personhood. Two adults may commit the same present act. One has never consummated a valid marriage and receives flogging; the other was married years earlier and may be stoned. The difference lies not in present harm but in legal biography.[127]

The problem is intensified by disagreement over what constitutes a valid marriage. A marriage may be valid under one school and defective under another, religiously recognized but not civilly registered, or civilly recognized but disputed by religious authorities. If iḥṣān activates death, the person's life depends upon which theory the state adopts.

Chastity and Conditional Dignity

In qadhf, full protection may depend upon chastity. A person whose prior zinā has been established may not receive the same protection against a new accusation. But a later falsehood remains false regardless of past conduct. A person may sin, serve a sentence, repent, reform, and rebuild life. Prior moral failure does not erase personhood or the right not to be falsely accused.[128]

Past reputation may properly affect proof of damages in a civil case. It should not determine whether a person possesses dignity at all. The

127 Bahnasi, Al-Ḥudūd fī al-Islām, section on zinā, on muḥṣan and non-muḥṣan status and disputed conditions activating stoning; Gabriel, "Reforming Hudud Ordinances," 95–97.

128Bahnasi, Al-Ḥudūd fī al-Islām, 99–139, on chastity as a condition of full fixed protection in qadhf.

classical condition transforms moral history into eligibility for legal protection.

Sanity, Age, and the Difference Between Culpability and Victimhood

Bahnasi records rules under which a person lacking sanity may not receive the same full qadhf protection, though discretionary punishment may remain. This confuses two different questions. Mental capacity is relevant to whether an accused person may be held responsible; it should not decide whether a victim deserves protection. Persons with mental disabilities may be especially vulnerable to ridicule, exploitation, and false accusation.[129]

Age presents a similar distinction. A child should not receive adult criminal punishment, but a false sexual accusation against a child may be exceptionally destructive. Modern law should protect children more strongly, not condition their dignity upon puberty or sexual capacity.

Bahnasi's recognition that the deceased may retain protected reputation because accusations harm lineage and surviving relatives is morally significant. Yet it sharpens the inconsistency of diminishing protection for living children, non-Muslims, enslaved persons, or persons with mental disabilities.

Testimonial Disqualification and Civil Degradation

The punishment for qadhf may include rejection of the accuser's future testimony. Jurists disagree over whether repentance restores testimonial competence. A lasting disqualification transforms the offender into a reduced legal participant who may be unable to testify even where he possesses accurate and essential knowledge.[130]

The classical concern is understandable: a person who made a grave unsupported accusation may be unreliable. But reliability is not the same as moral perfection. A morally flawed person may tell the truth, and a respected person may lie. Modern evidence law should assess

129Bahnasi, Al-Ḥudūd fī al-Islām, 99–139, on sanity and age among the conditions affecting the protected person in qadhf.

130Qur'an 24:4–5; Bahnasi, Al-Ḥudūd fī al-Islām, 99–139, on rejection of testimony and disagreement over restoration after repentance.

credibility in the particular case rather than impose permanent civil degradation.

Lineage, Birth, and Equal Childhood

The law of qadhf protects lineage because denying paternity or legitimate descent can produce grave social injury. Yet emphasis upon legitimate birth can reinforce inequality between children according to the conduct of their parents. A child does not choose the circumstances of conception. Equal legal personhood requires that every child possess the same status before the law.

Territory, Political Membership, and Conscience

Classical doctrine distinguished among Muslim territory, non-Muslim territory, protected communities, visitors, rebels, and persons outside ordinary jurisdiction. These categories belonged to a world of empires, religious communities, and differentiated political membership. A modern state claiming territorial jurisdiction over citizens and residents cannot reproduce them without creating layers of citizenship.

The doctrine of baghy may preserve protections for rebels, including limits on killing the wounded or taking family property. This restraint deserves acknowledgment. Yet the government still classifies opponents as dissenters, rebels, highway robbers, apostates, or ordinary criminals, and that classification determines legal status and punishment.

Apostasy represents the most radical status transformation. A person begins as a Muslim member of the community and, through belief, speech, or conduct classified as apostasy, may lose legal protection and become subject to death unless repentance occurs. Legal membership becomes conditional upon continued religious adherence. A person born Muslim did not choose the original status, yet the law may criminalize departure. This is incompatible with freedom of conscience and equal citizenship.[131]

131Gabriel, "Reforming Hudud Ordinances," 125–26, discussing discrimination based on religion and gender and the conflict between apostasy punishment and freedom of conscience.

The Modern Codifying State and Selective Restoration

A modern legislature attempting to restore the ḥudūd must decide whether to preserve historical distinctions or remove them. Preserving them produces explicit inequality. Removing them substantially alters the classical law. The legislature must decide whether non-Muslims receive equal qadhf protection, whether women's testimony equals men's, whether religious identity affects drinking liability, whether marital history still activates stoning, and how abolished slavery doctrines are treated.

The resulting code is necessarily a new construction. Restorationist projects often modernize status conditions while retaining bodily punishment. But if equality permits revision of classical personhood rules, proportionality and dignity must also permit revision of corporal sanctions. One cannot declare the tradition flexible everywhere except at the moment the body is cut, struck, or killed.

A state may remove slavery, religious inequality, exclusion of women, and historical territorial categories while preserving amputation, flogging, stoning, and execution. That is selective restoration: the social world is modernized while its harshest bodily penalties are retained. Such selection requires independent moral and constitutional justification.

Equality Is Necessary but Not Sufficient

The argument for equal personhood should not be dismissed as hostility toward Islam. Islamic moral teaching contains powerful affirmations of common human origin, individual accountability, justice, opposition to oppression, and moral worth before God. Modern constitutional equality can be understood as a legal expression of those values.

Yet a formally equal application of severe punishment would not solve the entire problem. A stoning law does not become just because it stones everyone equally. An amputation law does not become proportionate because religious distinctions are removed. Equality is necessary, but law must also be humane, proportionate, and institutionally legitimate.

Equal severity is not equal justice. True equality requires equal dignity, equal protection, equal evidentiary standing, equal access to counsel, and proportionate responsibility. It does not require equal exposure to mutilation.

The Universal Legal Person

A modern penal system should begin with one legal person whose rights do not depend upon religion, sex, ancestry, freedom status, marital history, chastity, disability, or social class. Equality does not eliminate responsibility. It attaches responsibility to conduct, harm, intention, consent, coercion, and culpability rather than inherited rank.

The legitimate purposes of the classical rules may be preserved within equal citizenship. Every person should receive equal protection against violence, theft, sexual assault, defamation, coercion, exploitation, and abuse of state power. Every accused person should receive presumption of innocence, equal evidentiary rules, counsel, impartial adjudication, appellate review, and protection from cruel or irreversible punishment.

Under this framework, theft protects every person's property while recognizing necessity and culpability; public violence is punished according to individual participation; sexual offenses are organized around consent and exploitation; defamation protects every person's reputation; alcohol law regulates concrete harm without religiously unequal liability; political opposition is distinguished from violence; and religious change remains protected conscience.

Conclusion

Bahnasi's penal order belongs to a historical world of differentiated legal personhood. Free and enslaved persons were not equal. Muslims and non-Muslims did not always receive identical protection. Men and women did not possess equal testimonial roles. Married and unmarried persons faced radically different punishment. Chaste and previously unchaste persons did not receive the same reputational protection. Children and persons with mental disabilities occupied distinct legal categories.

These rules may be studied historically and understood within their juristic setting. They should not be restored as the foundation of a modern criminal code. The central conclusion is direct:

> *Human dignity is not earned through religion, freedom, sex, chastity, marriage, or social rank. It belongs equally to every person.*

The offenses must therefore be reconstructed around conduct, harm, consent, culpability, and equal protection. The classical status hierarchy should not merely be softened. It should be left behind. The next chapter examines the physical means through which the classical system gives visible force to its authority.

Chapter Twelve

The Body as an Instrument of Deterrence and State Authority

The classical ḥudūd system gives the human body a central place within punishment. The body is cut, struck, restrained, exposed, displayed, and, in some cases, killed before others. These acts are not incidental to the sentence. They are the sentence. In Bahnasi's presentation, bodily punishment responds to the seriousness of the offense, deters the offender, warns the public, protects social order, and may contribute to spiritual expiation. The punishment becomes visible evidence that the law has been enforced.[132]

This distinguishes the ḥudūd from many modern penal forms. Imprisonment removes liberty, a fine removes wealth, and restitution addresses loss. Corporal punishment enters the body itself and leaves the judgment there. The removed hand remains absent for life. Cross-amputation permanently alters movement and work. Flogging deliberately produces pain. Stoning ends life through repeated bodily injury. Crucifixion turns the condemned or executed body into a public message.

That raises the fundamental question:

> *May the state use the human body as a permanent surface upon which it displays legal authority?*

Punishment Written upon the Body

Every punishment communicates. Corporal punishment communicates through pain and visible injury: the law has reached the offender, governing authority possesses power over the body, and observers should fear the same result. The body becomes both the recipient of punishment and the medium of public instruction.

Several classical punishments possess an apparent symbolic relationship to the offense. The hand is cut because it took property. The limbs are cut in ḥirāba because the offender combined appropriation

132 Bahnasi, Al-Ḥudūd fī al-Islām, discussions of bodily punishment, deterrence, and expiation.

with violent disruption. The body is flogged for sexual misconduct, accusation, or drinking. Crucifixion displays the defeat of one who challenged public order. This symbolism may appear morally symmetrical, but symbolism is not proportionality.

The body is also the means through which a person works, supports dependents, worships, communicates, travels, experiences pain, and rebuilds life. Bodily punishment therefore reaches far beyond the moment of the offense.

Amputation and Permanent State-Created Disability

Bahnasi's treatment of theft culminates in amputation once the technical conditions are satisfied. He discusses the anatomical location of the cut, repeated theft, and measures intended to prevent death from bleeding. The dominant rule identifies the right hand at the wrist for the first qualifying theft, while further cutting for repeated offenses remains disputed.[133]

Technical precision may reduce accidental death, but it cannot change the nature of the act. The state intentionally removes a functioning part of the body. The sentence continues after the wound closes through reduced earning capacity, difficulty with daily tasks, chronic pain, infection, psychological trauma, stigma, dependence, and hardship imposed upon innocent family members.

No criminal process is infallible. Mistaken identity, false testimony, disputed ownership, coerced confession, incorrect valuation, or error concerning protected custody may lead to wrongful conviction. Later acquittal cannot restore a hand. Irreversibility transforms judicial error into permanent state-created disability.

In ḥirāba, the Qur'anic alternatives include cutting the hand and opposite foot. Bahnasi presents cross-amputation where property is taken without killing. The sentence deliberately destroys balance, mobility, work capacity, and independence. A constitutional order committed to equal dignity should not manufacture disability as a penal objective or public warning.[134]

---

133 Bahnasi, Al-Ḥudūd fī al-Islām, 61–90, on amputation, repeat theft, and measures intended to prevent fatal bleeding.

134 Qur'an 5:33; Bahnasi, Al-Ḥudūd fī al-Islām, section on ḥirāba and the differentiated penalties of killing, crucifixion, cross-amputation,

Flogging and the Regulation of Pain

Flogging appears in the doctrines of zinā, qadhf, drinking, and other offenses. Jurists regulate the number of lashes, instrument, force, distribution of blows, clothing, bodily areas, illness, pregnancy, and postponement. These rules demonstrate concern with preventing death or excessive injury. Yet the purpose of the sentence remains the intentional infliction of pain.[135]

The number may appear fixed while suffering is not. Pain varies according to instrument, strength of the person striking, condition of the skin, age and health of the accused, spacing of blows, and bodily areas reached. Equal numerical punishment therefore produces unequal physical experience.

Postponement for pregnancy or illness contains a revealing contradiction. The punishment is judged too dangerous for a vulnerable body, yet legitimate once that body becomes strong enough to endure it.

Stoning and Collective Killing

Bahnasi defines stoning as killing the muḥṣan offender through repeated throwing of stones. He discusses who begins the punishment, the role of the ruler and witnesses, and differences between convictions based upon testimony and confession. Stoning combines execution, prolonged injury, humiliation, public participation, and collective responsibility.[136]

The method does not guarantee immediate unconsciousness or rapid death. The condemned person may experience terror, fractures, bleeding, repeated pain, and gradual physical collapse. Stones also

---

and banishment; Gabriel, "Reforming Hudud Ordinances," 49–50, 196–99.

135 Bahnasi, Al-Ḥudūd fī al-Islām, discussions of flogging in the sections on zinā, qadhf, and intoxicants, including number, instrument, bodily condition, and postponement. See also Gabriel, "Reforming Hudud Ordinances," 95–100, 124–26, 183–92.

136 Bahnasi, Al-Ḥudūd fī al-Islām, section on zinā, on stoning, confession, witness involvement, and retraction; Gabriel, "Reforming Hudud Ordinances," 97–100, 183–86.

disperse responsibility: no participant may identify a single fatal act, and the community kills through accumulation.

Where witnesses begin the stoning, participation may be presented as a final test of certainty. But testimony should be tested before sentence through cross-examination, corroboration, consistency, and independent review, not by requiring witnesses to assist in killing.

The disagreement over a confessor who attempts to flee makes the danger unmistakable. If confession established guilt and the person withdraws after stoning begins, jurists differ over whether participants must stop. Such uncertainty is incompatible with capital punishment.

Crucifixion, Display, and Dignity after Death

In ḥirāba, Bahnasi presents crucifixion in connection with the gravest forms of violent public crime. Jurists differ over whether the offender is crucified before or after death and over the duration and manner of display. Execution ends capacity to harm; crucifixion adds humiliation, warning, and political spectacle.[137]

The displayed body becomes a sign of the ruler's power and the defeat of the offender. Human dignity should not disappear at death. A body should not become state property for public degradation.

Public Spectacle and Deterrence

The public dimension appears repeatedly. The Qur'an directs that a group of believers witness flogging for zinā. Stoning may involve witnesses, officials, and community members. Crucifixion displays the offender, and amputation leaves a visible permanent mark.[138]

Public punishment requires an audience. The state uses the offender's pain, fear, body, and shame to influence others. The possible deterrent effect of fear does not establish legitimacy. Deterrence must remain bounded by dignity, proportionality, equality, and rights.

The classical system contains a paradox: severe punishments are highly visible in threat, while doctrines of doubt and strict proof often

---

137 Bahnasi, Al-Ḥudūd fī al-Islām, section on ḥirāba, on crucifixion and public punishment; see also Gabriel, "Reforming Hudud Ordinances," 49–50, 196–99.

138 Qur'an 24:2; Bahnasi, Al-Ḥudūd fī al-Islām, on public witnessing of flogging and the deterrent function of visible punishment.

avoid their actual use. The system may depend more upon the image of bodily punishment than upon frequent enforcement.

Public punishment may also injure observers. Children and other members of the community may witness blood, whipping, mutilation, humiliation, or death. The intended lesson is respect for law; the actual lesson may be trauma or normalization of violence.

Sacralized Violence and the Disappearance of Responsibility

The danger increases when governments use punishment to display religious legitimacy. A ruler may stage flogging, amputation, or execution as proof of commitment to Islamic law, control over morality, or strength against crime. The convicted body then authenticates the regime.

When corporal punishment is described as the right of God, officials may deny human choice. The court invokes the statute; the legislature invokes jurists; jurists invoke revelation; the executioner invokes obedience. Yet every step remains human: someone selects the rule, establishes facts, signs the judgment, restrains the accused, strikes, cuts, throws, and certifies death.[139]

A modern state must own its coercion. Whenever it restrains, imprisons, injures, or kills, it must justify that act through legality, necessity, evidence, equality, proportionality, and constitutional review. Divine attribution cannot replace institutional accountability.

Expiation and the Limits of State Competence

Bahnasi connects worldly punishment with the possibility of spiritual expiation. Within personal faith, voluntary penance may carry meaning. The state, however, cannot know whether repentance is sincere, whether God has forgiven, whether bodily suffering purifies, or whether divine mercy has already intervened.[140]

---

139 Bahnasi, Al-Ḥudūd fī al-Islām, presenting the ḥudūd as rights of God and fixed punishments; Wael B. Hallaq, Shari'a: Theory, Practice, Transformations (Cambridge: Cambridge University Press, 2009).

140 Bahnasi, Al-Ḥudūd fī al-Islām, 10–17, on punishment as expiation and purification in the religious theory of punishment.

There is a fundamental difference between voluntary spiritual discipline and forced bodily injury. The first may be an act of conscience. The second is coercion.

Bodily Integrity, Medicine, and Institutional Morality

Bodily integrity is foundational because the body is the physical condition through which every other right is exercised. The state may use proportionate force to prevent immediate violence or protect others. Punitive mutilation is different: it is retrospective injury inflicted after the accused is under control.

Medical involvement does not resolve the problem. A physician may determine whether an offender can survive, whether pregnancy or illness requires postponement, where cutting may occur, or whether death has resulted. Medical knowledge then becomes a means of making injury survivable rather than preventing it.

The system also requires officials to bind, strike, cut, throw, or display. Those officials may experience psychological harm, desensitization, moral conflict, or normalization of cruelty.

Permanent Stigma, Proportionality, and Reversibility

Amputation creates a visible record that may announce conviction throughout life. This undermines repentance and rehabilitation. The system may speak of purification while ensuring permanent social stigma.

Fixed bodily punishments also limit proportionality. The same amputation may follow thefts of substantially different value once a threshold is crossed; the same lashes may apply despite differing motives and harms; and the same death sentence may apply to private sexual conduct without violence.

Reversibility is essential because human institutions make mistakes, evidence changes, and witnesses recant. A wrongfully imprisoned person may be released. A wrongfully amputated person cannot recover the limb, and a wrongfully executed person cannot receive any remedy. The trial, witnesses, codification, and enforcement remain human even when the underlying rule is presented as divine.[141]

---

141 Mark A. Gabriel, "Reforming Hudud Ordinances to Reconcile Islamic Criminal Law with International Human Rights Law" (PhD

Spectacle, Hierarchy, and Social Failure

Public bodily punishment is especially dangerous under authoritarian government. It can intimidate opponents, demonstrate religious legitimacy, enforce conformity, and display control over marginalized groups. The bodies most likely to be punished may belong to the poor, migrants, women, minorities, political opponents, or persons without effective counsel.

Petty theft, private morality, and public intoxication may be easy to prosecute, while corruption, financial abuse, and state violence remain protected by power. Corporal punishment can mutilate the weak while greater social harms remain untouched.

The state may punish an individual body while ignoring poverty, addiction, abuse, unemployment, mental illness, and institutional corruption. Visible suffering creates an appearance of order and may conceal governmental failure to address causes.

A Constructive Alternative

Rejecting bodily punishment does not require abandoning accountability. Restitution, compensation, proportionate detention, supervised release, treatment, rehabilitation, protective orders, and disqualification from particular activities can punish, deter, repair, and protect without mutilating the body. Grave violence may require secure restraint, but loss of liberty need not become public degradation.

Restorative justice directs attention toward the victim's loss, the offender's responsibility, repair of harm, and prevention of recurrence. Amputation does not restore stolen property. Flogging does not restore reputation. Stoning does not repair a marriage. Crucifixion does not compensate victims.

The moral authority of a powerful state is shown not by the severity of injuries it can inflict, but by the restraint it exercises when it possesses power. Society may condemn theft, violence, betrayal, false accusation, intoxication, and political violence with complete seriousness. It does not need to write condemnation upon the body.[142]

---

diss., University of Cape Town, 2016), on amputation, flogging, stoning, human fallibility, and irreversibility.

142 Gabriel, "Reforming Hudud Ordinances," concluding reform proposals; Mohammad Hashim Kamali, Shariah Law: An

Conclusion

The classical ḥudūd establish a political relationship between governing authority and the human body. Bahnasi's detailed treatment of instruments, numbers, anatomical locations, postponement, participation, and public witnessing demonstrates serious concern with limiting excessive injury. But careful administration does not answer the foundational issue.

A carefully administered mutilation remains mutilation. A regulated flogging remains deliberate pain. A procedurally organized stoning remains death by collective bodily violence. A postmortem crucifixion remains public degradation.

The conclusion follows:

> *The human body should not serve as the permanent canvas upon which the modern state writes its moral authority.*

The state may restrain dangerous persons, protect victims, require restitution, impose proportionate punishment, and defend public safety. It should not manufacture disability, stage pain, or turn death into public instruction. A lawful state should be known not by the severity of the injuries it can inflict, but by the discipline with which it limits its own power. The next chapter moves from bodily authority to political authority.

Introduction (Oxford: Oneworld, 2008).

Chapter Thirteen

Rebellion and the State's Claim to Sacred Legitimacy

The classical doctrine of baghy, or rebellion, addresses a real political danger: organized armed resistance capable of bloodshed, fragmentation, and destruction of the institutions necessary for public order. No legal system can ignore violent insurrection. Government must be able to protect citizens, restore peace, and prevent armed groups from imposing their will by force. Yet rebellion differs from ordinary crime because the state is itself the authority being resisted. It becomes the alleged victim, the interpreter of lawful obedience, the classifier of opposition, the prosecutor, and the institution authorized to suppress the accused group.[143]

That concentration of roles creates a constitutional danger:

> *The state may transform resistance to its political authority into an offense against divine order.*

Bahnasi's treatment of baghy contains important restraints. Rebels may remain Muslims rather than enemies outside the community. They may act from a claimed interpretation, possess organized strength, and be treated under rules limiting vengeance against prisoners, wounded persons, families, and property. Those protections deserve recognition. But they do not answer the foundational question: who determines that the ruler is legitimate and the resistance unlawful?

The Definition of Baghy

Bahnasi defines rebels as a group of Muslims who depart from obedience to the imam, possess collective strength, and act upon an interpretation they regard as supporting their position. Their power is sufficient that ordinary arrest is inadequate and organized force may be

143 Aḥmad Fatḥī Bahnasi, Al-Ḥudūd fī al-Islām, Shuʿāʿ al-Islām no. 12 (Alexandria: Muʾassasat Shabāb al-Jāmiʿa, n.d.), section on al-baghy; see also Gabriel, "Reforming Hudud Ordinances," 93–95, 109–10, on the classical overlap between rebellion, ḥirāba, and public violence.

required. The definition therefore combines political disobedience, collective organization, claimed interpretation, and actual capacity to resist.[144]

Each element requires human judgment. A ruler or court must decide whether the group's argument is plausible, whether its strength is genuinely military, and whether its conduct threatens public order. The offense is not established merely because violence occurred; the state must classify the political and intellectual character of the movement.

The Unresolved Assumption of a Legitimate Imam

The doctrine begins with an imam whose obedience is legally required. Yet political legitimacy was never historically self-evident. Muslim rulers came to power through consultation, designation, inheritance, military conquest, revolution, palace struggle, and eventual recognition after seizure of power. The modern state presents still more possibilities: monarchy, elected presidency, military rule, parliament, party government, revolutionary authority, or a constitutional order divided among institutions.

Effective control is not moral legitimacy. A government may possess power while suppressing elections, imprisoning opponents, violating the constitution, or using public institutions for private and sectarian interests. If possession of power automatically creates a duty of obedience, successful coercion becomes its own justification.

The Qur'anic Priority of Reconciliation

Bahnasi relies upon Qur'an 49:9, which addresses two groups of believers who fight one another. The community is instructed first to reconcile them; if one group persists in aggression, it is resisted until it returns to the command of God; after return, reconciliation must be established with justice and fairness.[145]

---

144 Bahnasi, Al-Ḥudūd fī al-Islām, section on al-baghy, defining rebellion through departure from obedience, collective power, and a claimed interpretation (taʾwīl). See also Gabriel, "Reforming Hudud Ordinances," 93–95, 109–10.

145 Qur'an 49:9. The verse first commands reconciliation between two fighting groups of believers, then limited resistance to the

The sequence is decisive. The verse begins with reconciliation, not punishment. Both groups remain believers. Force is directed toward ending aggression, not exterminating political enemies. Justice remains required after the aggressing party returns. The text therefore does not grant unlimited sacred authority to every ruler.

The modern legal lesson is strong: dialogue, mediation, negotiation, constitutional remedy, and peaceful settlement should precede coercion whenever possible. If force becomes necessary, its purpose is to stop violence and restore lawful peace, not to create permanent enemies.

Ta'wīl and Political Disagreement

A claimed interpretation, or ta'wīl, distinguishes rebels from ordinary bandits acting solely for private gain. This recognizes that political conflict may arise from sincere disagreement rather than criminal appetite. Yet the protection depends upon the fairness of the authority whose position is challenged. An authoritarian government may dismiss every constitutional objection as fabricated or extremist.[146]

Political movements also contain mixed motives. Some participants may seek justice, others power; some may be coerced, others peaceful supporters associated with a violent faction. The state cannot assign one intention to an entire movement. Individual responsibility must remain central.

Power, Organization, and the Protection of Peaceful Opposition

Bahnasi associates baghy with organized strength, a defended position or territory, and, according to some views, a leader. These requirements distinguish civil conflict from isolated disobedience and can protect ordinary dissent. A critic, scholar, journalist, political party, or peaceful mass movement does not become a rebel merely by challenging those in office.[147]

---

aggressing group until it returns, followed by reconciliation with justice.

146 Bahnasi, Al-Ḥudūd fī al-Islām, section on al-baghy, on ta'wīl as a feature distinguishing rebels from ordinary criminals or bandits; see also Gabriel, "Reforming Hudud Ordinances," 93–95.

Modern governments may nevertheless redefine power broadly to include popular support, communication networks, fundraising, demonstrations, or international visibility. Political influence is not armed power. Any modern statute must preserve a bright line between peaceful organization and violent insurrection.

The Humane Restraints in the Classical Doctrine

Bahnasi records rules limiting the treatment of rebels: the wounded should not be killed, fugitives should not be pursued once danger has ended, prisoners should not be executed merely for participation, families should not be enslaved, and property should not be divided as spoils. The objective is to terminate rebellion, not annihilate the opposing group.[148]

These principles contain enduring value. Even during armed conflict, government must distinguish active fighters, prisoners, wounded persons, noncombatants, families, and property. Collective punishment is illegitimate. Force must end when the danger ends.

Fighting Is Not the Same as Execution

The Qur'anic instruction to fight an aggressing group until it returns does not necessarily authorize execution after surrender. Once aggression ceases, the stated objective has been achieved. A modern system must distinguish defensive force used during active conflict from punitive killing after capture.

Bahnasi's compressed discussion leaves major questions unresolved: how legitimacy is established, how peaceful opposition is protected, who independently evaluates taʾwīl, how individual

---

147 Bahnasi, Al-Ḥudūd fī al-Islām, section on al-baghy, on collective strength, defended position, leadership, and the practical distinction between isolated disobedience and organized rebellion. For the broader classical treatment of rebellion, see Gabriel, "Reforming Hudud Ordinances," 93–95, 109–10.

148 Bahnasi, Al-Ḥudūd fī al-Islām, section on al-baghy, on restrictions governing force against rebels and protection of persons and property after hostilities. See also Qur'an 49:9 and Gabriel, "Reforming Hudud Ordinances," 109–10, on reconciliation and limited force against a transgressing group.

participation is proven, when governmental violence becomes unlawful, and what remedy exists against tyranny. These questions determine whether the doctrine protects order or merely protects power.

Order, Tyranny, and Peaceful Opposition

Order is valuable because it protects human beings and enables justice. It is not identical to justice. A dictatorship may maintain stability through repression, and a corrupt ruler may suppress opposition while violating law. Classical caution toward rebellion reflected the real fear that revolt could produce greater bloodshed than the injustice opposed, but prudential caution cannot become divine immunity for government.

A modern constitutional order must distinguish peaceful criticism, protest, voting, political organization, civil disobedience, whistleblowing, journalism, and demands for constitutional change from armed insurrection. Only genuine violence or an imminent violent threat should activate extraordinary security law.[149]

Individual Responsibility and the Danger of Collective Guilt

A movement may include leaders, armed participants, medics, negotiators, journalists, family members, coerced supporters, and civilians trapped in territory under rebel control. Membership or proximity cannot establish equal guilt. The conduct and intention of each accused person must be proven.

Political advocacy must also be distinguished from direct incitement to immediate violence. Calling for a government to resign or for a constitutional system to change is political speech. Organizing an imminent armed attack is a different legal act.

Emergency Power and Independent Adjudication

Rebellion prosecutions create an institutional conflict of interest. State security forces gather evidence, state prosecutors bring charges, state courts adjudicate, and the executive carries out punishment. Emergency

---

149 Gabriel, “Reforming Hudud Ordinances,” 93–95, 109–10, 196–99, on the need to distinguish violent public offenses from political disagreement and to constrain coercive authority.

powers may expand detention, secrecy, intelligence evidence, and military jurisdiction precisely when political pressure is greatest.

Independent courts must therefore examine not only the opposition's conduct but also the legality of governmental action, the existence of genuine violence, individual participation, and the proportionality of force. Qur'an 49:9 does not assume that government can never be the aggressor. State forces may initiate unlawful violence, attack peaceful demonstrators, torture detainees, or provoke conflict.[150]

The Sacralization of the Regime

The danger reaches its highest point when a ruler identifies himself with the imam, the imam with divine order, and opposition to his government with rebellion against God. Political survival then becomes a sacred interest. This is not divine government; it is human power shielded by theological language.

The community, nation, religion, and governing regime are not identical. A regime may fall while society survives. Officials may change while the constitutional order continues. Criticism of government is not hostility toward Islam, and opposition to one political arrangement is not necessarily opposition to the community.

From Personal Obedience to Constitutional Loyalty

The modern state is not embodied in one imam. It includes constitutions, legislatures, courts, bureaucracies, national armies, police, elections, parties, and internationally recognized citizenship. Authority is divided. Consequently, departure from obedience to the imam cannot be transferred directly into modern criminal language.

The proper object of political loyalty is the lawful constitutional order, not the ruler's person. Officials remain subject to law and may be challenged, removed, or replaced through lawful institutions. Modern offenses such as treason, armed insurrection, conspiracy, terrorism, murder, kidnapping, and attacks upon constitutional institutions can be

---

150 Qur'an 49:9; the text requires identification of the aggressing party and justice after hostilities, a structure that does not place governmental conduct beyond review.

defined through conduct without declaring political opponents enemies of God.[151]

Reconciliation, Accountability, and Reintegration

The strongest constructive principle in the classical doctrine is reconciliation. Civil conflict destroys communities beyond the battlefield. Responsible government should seek ceasefire, mediation, disarmament, truth-telling, accountability for grave crimes, and reintegration. Conditional amnesty may be appropriate for participants who did not commit murder, torture, kidnapping, or comparable atrocities, while victims' rights remain protected.

The classical restraints should therefore be preserved within constitutional and humanitarian law: do not kill the wounded, execute prisoners merely for affiliation, pursue those who have ceased fighting without necessity, enslave families, or seize property as spoils. But these protections must be separated from a sacralized theory of obedience.

A Constructive Modern Alternative

A modern framework should rest upon constitutional legitimacy, protected peaceful opposition, precise definitions of armed insurrection, individualized responsibility, independent adjudication, necessary and proportionate force, protection of noncombatants and detainees, negotiation before escalation, and accountability for governmental as well as opposition violence.[152]

This framework protects public order without placing the regime beyond challenge. It preserves the classical concern for reconciliation and restraint while refusing to treat political obedience as a divine right.

---

151 Wael B. Hallaq, Shari'a: Theory, Practice, Transformations (Cambridge: Cambridge University Press, 2009), on the historical institutional setting of classical Islamic law and the transformation produced by modern state codification; Mohammad Hashim Kamali, Shariah Law: An Introduction (Oxford: Oneworld, 2008), on constitutional governance, public interest, and legal restraint.

152 Gabriel, "Reforming Hudud Ordinances," 160–99, on constitutional safeguards, individualized responsibility, proportionality, doubt, and human-rights-compatible alternatives.

Conclusion

Bahnasi's treatment of baghy is brief, but its implications are profound. It recognizes that political rebels may remain members of the community, act from a claimed interpretation, and receive protections against vengeance and extermination. Those restraints demonstrate juristic awareness of the complexity of civil conflict.

Yet the doctrine begins from an unresolved assumption: the legitimacy of the ruler. In the modern state, that legitimacy cannot be declared by the ruler himself. It must be constitutional, accountable, and open to peaceful challenge.

The conclusion follows:

> *No government should be permitted to convert political obedience into a right of God or to classify resistance to its own authority as rebellion against divine order.*

Violent insurrection may be punished. Murder, terrorism, kidnapping, and destruction may be prosecuted. But peaceful opposition must remain protected, and government itself must remain subject to law. The state may defend the constitutional order. It may not sacralize the regime. The next chapter examines the final and most direct claim of state authority over conscience.

Chapter Fourteen

Apostasy, Religious Freedom, and the Criminalization of Conscience

Bahnasi ends his substantive treatment of the ḥudūd with apostasy. The placement is significant. His book moves from offenses involving property, public violence, sexual morality, reputation, and intoxication to an offense directed toward religious identity itself. Here the state does not merely judge what a person has done. It judges what the person believes, whether the person still belongs to Islam, and whether a change of conviction may be answered with imprisonment or death.

Bahnasi defines apostasy linguistically as returning from one condition to another and legally as departure from Islam. He cites Qur'anic passages condemning those who turn away from faith and relies upon prophetic reports for a worldly death penalty. He requires the alleged apostate to be Muslim, adult, sane, and acting voluntarily; discusses istitāba, the invitation to repent; and records disagreement over delay, immediate execution, and the treatment of women. His concise account brings together nearly every difficulty examined in the preceding chapters: movement from spiritual condemnation to state punishment, juristic construction, procedural disagreement, coercion presented as mercy, unequal legal status, and the transfer of religious authority to government.

The decisive issue is not whether apostasy may carry theological or moral consequences within Islam. The decisive issue is:

> *Should any government possess authority to imprison, beat, or kill a human being merely for leaving a religion?*

Defining Apostasy and Judging the Interior Life

Apostasy appears simple when described merely as departure from Islam. Its legal application is not. A person may declare conversion openly, but apostasy may also be alleged through denial of doctrine, criticism of scripture, rejection of an obligation, words regarded as insulting, participation in another religion, philosophical disbelief, conduct interpreted as incompatible with faith, or refusal to affirm an official theological position. A court must therefore decide not only whether religious affiliation changed but what counts as Islam and what places a person outside it.

Government thereby becomes a theological judge. It must identify indispensable doctrines, distinguish doubt from unbelief, determine whether satire or criticism demonstrates departure, and infer inward conviction from outward language. Those questions have divided theologians and jurists for centuries. A criminal court cannot determine the condition of the human heart with the certainty required for any punishment, much less death.

Belief is not directly observable. Government can examine speech, writing, ritual conduct, association, and public declaration. It cannot observe faith itself. A scholar may investigate an argument without personally accepting it. A believer may doubt without abandoning religion. A critic may oppose a religious institution while remaining Muslim. The state cannot know the heart.

Voluntariness Does Not Make Conscience Criminal

Bahnasi requires adulthood, sanity, and voluntariness. These conditions are consistent with general principles of responsibility, but they answer only whether the religious departure was chosen knowingly. They do not answer why a voluntary change of religion should be a crime. Indeed, the more sincere and voluntary the change, the more clearly punishment is directed against conscience itself.[153]

Bahnasi also cites the Qur'anic protection of the person compelled to pronounce unbelief while the heart remains secure in faith. This distinction between outward speech and inward conviction is important, but it undermines the state's claim to judge belief. If the heart may remain faithful while the tongue speaks unbelief, the tongue may also proclaim faith while the heart no longer believes. Government can compel words; it cannot compel conviction.[154]

---

153 Bahnasi, Al-Ḥudūd fī al-Islām, apostasy section, including the definition of riddah and conditions of legal responsibility; Gabriel, "Reforming Hudud Ordinances," 46–48, 110–12.

154 Qur'an 16:106; Bahnasi, Al-Ḥudūd fī al-Islām, apostasy section, on voluntariness and coercion. For the broader classical

Qur'anic Condemnation and the Absence of a Stated Worldly Sentence

The Qur'anic passages concerning apostasy speak of divine anger, loss of deeds, spiritual failure, and punishment in the hereafter. They present apostasy as a grave religious matter, but spiritual judgment is not the same as a state-administered criminal sentence. A text may declare that God will judge without authorizing government to kill.[155]

The Qur'an also describes persons who believe, disbelieve, believe again, and then disbelieve. That sequence presupposes continued earthly life after more than one change. It sits uneasily with execution after the first legally established departure. The future in which a person may reconsider and return should not be eliminated by the state.

The principle that there is no compulsion in religion cannot be confined to entry into faith. A religion is not freely embraced where entry is permitted but departure is punishable by death. Religious freedom requires the ability to adopt conviction and the ability to change it.

The Hadith Evidence and Historical Context

Bahnasi relies principally upon the report, "Whoever changes his religion, kill him," and the report permitting the blood of the Muslim who abandons religion and separates from the community. Both require interpretation. The first is extraordinarily broad if separated from its communal and historical setting, yet classical law did not apply it symmetrically to every person changing any religion. The juristic limitation itself demonstrates that interpretation was already necessary.[156]

---

framework of apostasy liability, see Gabriel, "Reforming Hudud Ordinances," 110–12.

155 See Qur'an 2:217; 3:86–91; 4:137; and 16:106. These passages emphasize divine and otherworldly consequences without stating a worldly death sentence for peaceful religious change. See also Gabriel, "Reforming Hudud Ordinances," 46–48, 74–76, 176–80.

156 Bahnasi, Al-Ḥudūd fī al-Islām, apostasy section, relying upon the reports commonly rendered as "Whoever changes his religion, kill him" and the Muslim who "abandons his religion and separates from the community." For a critical examination of the hadith evidence, see

The second report is particularly significant because it links religious departure with separation from the community. In the early Muslim polity, religion, political allegiance, military obligation, and communal membership were closely connected. Apostasy could coincide with hostile defection, rebellion, alliance with an enemy, or refusal of public obligations. Those acts must be distinguished from peaceful intellectual or religious change.

A person who joins an enemy force, commits espionage, organizes violence, or wages war may properly be prosecuted for treason, conspiracy, rebellion, or violence. Changing belief is not itself the harmful act. A peaceful former Muslim is not legally equivalent to a person who defects during war and joins an armed enemy. Historical fusion of religious and political membership does not justify their permanent fusion in modern criminal law.

Istitāba and Coercion Presented as Mercy

Bahnasi presents istitāba as an invitation to return to Islam before punishment. One view allows detention for three days while the accused is repeatedly invited to repent. Another does not require a waiting period and permits execution once apostasy is established, although repentance offered immediately may be accepted. The procedural path to death is therefore not uniform.[157]

The three-day period is often presented as mercy, but the context cannot be ignored. The person is not participating in open theological dialogue. The choice is return to Islam or be killed. That is coercion. A profession of faith made under threat of death establishes fear, not conviction.

The procedure rewards outward dishonesty over inward honesty. The person who truthfully acknowledges disbelief faces death, while the person who falsely declares renewed belief survives. A law intended to protect religion therefore encourages hypocrisy. The state may obtain conformity, recitation, or silence. It cannot restore faith.

Gabriel, "Reforming Hudud Ordinances," 176–80.

157 Bahnasi, Al-Ḥudūd fī al-Islām, apostasy section, on istitāba, the waiting period attributed to some authorities, and execution following refusal to return; Gabriel, "Reforming Hudud Ordinances," 110–12.

The Female Apostate and Unequal Coercion

Bahnasi records a major disagreement regarding women. The majority position applies death to men and women after the opportunity for repentance. The Ḥanafī position does not execute the female apostate but subjects her to confinement and pressure, including beating, until she returns. The distinction suggests that the death penalty may have been connected partly to perceived political and military danger rather than belief alone.[158]

The Ḥanafī rule avoids execution, but imprisonment and bodily pressure remain incompatible with religious freedom. The disagreement concerns the method of coercion, not whether conscience may be coerced. A modern government selecting between death and indefinite pressure would be making a legislative and political choice, not mechanically applying one uncontested divine rule.

Inherited Identity and the One-Way Gate

Apostasy law also treats inherited religious identity as a binding legal status. One person may have voluntarily entered Islam as an adult; another may have been classified as Muslim from birth without ever choosing that identity. Both may be treated as having abandoned an irrevocable obligation.

No person chooses parents, birthplace, childhood community, or official religious registration. Birth cannot create a permanent religious contract enforceable by imprisonment or death. Apostasy law creates a one-way gate: entry into Islam is permitted and encouraged, while departure is prohibited. That is expansion without exit, not reciprocal freedom.

Speech, Scholarship, and Sectarian Power

Where apostasy may be established by speech, the law threatens theologians, historians, writers, artists, philosophers, reformers, and

---

158 Bahnasi, Al-Ḥudūd fī al-Islām, apostasy section, on disagreement concerning the female apostate, including the majority position of execution and the Ḥanafī position of confinement rather than immediate execution; Gabriel, "Reforming Hudud Ordinances," 111–12.

ordinary believers expressing doubt. A statement may be removed from context; a metaphor may be misunderstood; a scholarly hypothesis may be treated as a personal confession. The threat of punishment produces self-censorship.

The problem has direct relevance to this study. A scholar who questions stoning, amputation, apostasy, a claimed consensus, or the authority of modern governments may be accused of denying Islam itself. Apostasy law can therefore shield the inherited penal order from examination and become the final enforcement mechanism of doctrinal conformity.

Islamic history contains deep disagreement among Sunni and Shiʿi traditions, rationalists and traditionalists, philosophers, mystics, and competing legal schools. A government empowered to punish apostasy must decide which theology is official. Minority interpretations become vulnerable, and a law presented as protection of religion becomes sectarian law.

Political Use and Social Violence

Governments may recast political criticism as hostility to Islam, insult to religion, dissemination of unbelief, or attack upon the religious foundations of the state. The ruler then protects political authority through theological prosecution. Even where formal execution is rare, an accusation of apostasy may expose a person to family violence, social exclusion, employment loss, divorce, loss of custody, threats, or vigilante attack.

State criminalization legitimizes these dangers by communicating that the accused has lost ordinary protection. A religious community may make internal judgments concerning membership, ritual participation, religious office, and teaching. Those judgments should not remove citizenship, bodily protection, property, family rights, access to courts, or life.

The State Cannot Administer Salvation

Within religious belief, the ultimate consequence of apostasy belongs to God. Bahnasi's Qur'anic citations themselves emphasize divine judgment and the hereafter. Government has no authority to accelerate that judgment by killing the person. It is institutionally capable of investigating violence, property loss, or threats, though even those determinations are fallible. It is far less capable of deciding whether faith is genuine, doubt has become disbelief, repentance is sincere, or God has forgiven.

Execution also ends the moral journey in which a person might reconsider, return, develop another understanding, or remain outside the faith. A state claiming to defend religion should not destroy the future in which persuasion and conscience may still operate.

Freedom of Conscience and the Security Distinction

Freedom of conscience protects the moral agency to believe, disbelieve, question, convert, return, worship, abstain from worship, and change conviction. It does not assert that all beliefs are theologically true. It asserts that government should not decide religious truth through coercion. International human-rights law similarly protects the freedom to have or adopt a religion or belief of one's choice and prohibits coercion impairing that freedom.[159]

Religious freedom does not protect violence. A person who joins an armed enemy, commits treason, incites imminent attack, funds terrorism, or participates in rebellion may be prosecuted for that conduct. But government must prove the harmful act independently. Apostasy cannot serve as a substitute for evidence of a security offense.

The constructive distinction is therefore clear: punish violence, espionage, armed collaboration, incitement, and material participation in crime; protect conversion, doubt, criticism, worship, nonbelief, and peaceful religious association.

Plural Citizenship and the Right to Silence

A modern nation may include Muslims, Christians, Jews, adherents of other religions, former believers, and persons without religious affiliation. Citizenship must remain stable through changes of belief. Otherwise, religion becomes a condition of political membership and the state ceases to be a common legal home.

Freedom of conscience also includes the right not to disclose inner belief. A person should not be compelled to answer whether faith

---

159International Covenant on Civil and Political Rights, art. 18(1)-(2), 999 U.N.T.S. 171; see also art. 26 on equal protection without discrimination.

remains, which doctrines are accepted, whether conversion occurred, or whether repentance is sincere. Apostasy proceedings turn conscience itself into evidence.

Why Procedural Reform Is Not Enough

The problem cannot be solved merely by replacing death with imprisonment, a fine, or a longer repentance period. Any state punishment imposed solely for peaceful religious change remains illegitimate. Stricter evidence, appellate review, psychiatric assessment, or restriction to public declaration may reduce error, but they cannot make conscience a proper criminal object.

This distinguishes peaceful apostasy from conduct involving tangible harm. The offense itself, not merely the severity of the sentence, must be removed from criminal law. Gabriel's earlier doctoral research likewise concluded that neither the Qur'an nor reliable evidence of prophetic practice supplies sufficient justification for a worldly death penalty for peaceful departure from Islam and argued that apostasy should not be treated as a ḥadd crime.[160]

A Constructive Alternative

A Muslim-majority state may protect religious life without punishing departure. It may protect places of worship, permit religious education, prevent coercive conversion, punish violence against believers, defend peaceful preaching, prohibit discrimination, and secure equal freedom for every community.

Religious institutions may teach the theological seriousness of apostasy and invite return through argument, compassion, example, and pastoral care. They should not employ police, imprisonment, beating, or execution. The proper response to doubt is dialogue; the proper response to criticism is argument; the proper response to conversion is freedom; and the proper response to violence is law directed toward the violence.

160Mark A. Gabriel, 'Reforming Hudud Ordinances to Reconcile Islamic Criminal Law with International Human Rights Law' (PhD diss., University of Cape Town, 2016), 176-80.

Conclusion

Bahnasi treats apostasy as departure from Islam by a legally responsible and voluntary Muslim. He cites Qur'anic condemnation, relies upon prophetic reports for worldly execution, discusses invitation to repentance, and records disagreement over delay and the treatment of women. His concise account nevertheless requires extensive human construction: which words establish apostasy, how inward belief is inferred, whether repentance must be offered, how long government must wait, whether execution may be immediate, and whether women are killed or coerced by other means.[161]

Apostasy brings the problem of the ḥudūd to its most revealing point. The state no longer protects a victim from violence, theft, or defamation. It protects a religious boundary against the person's own conscience and claims authority to determine belief, demand repentance, restrain the dissenter, and take life.

No modern state should possess that authority. A person who commits violence or treason may be punished for violence or treason. A person who peacefully changes religion should remain fully protected as a citizen and human being. The central principle is therefore:

> *Conscience cannot be made a prison, and faith cannot be made a condition of survival.*

Islam may remain a source of moral teaching, communal identity, spiritual truth, and public ethical reflection. But no state, regime, or armed movement claiming to enforce Islamic criminal law should use death or bodily coercion to preserve belief. The next chapter draws together the institutional argument that has emerged across all the offenses.

---

161 Bahnasi, Al-Ḥudūd fī al-Islām, apostasy section, on legal capacity, voluntariness, repentance, waiting period, execution, and disagreement concerning women; Gabriel, "Reforming Hudud Ordinances," 110–12. No precise Bahnasi page number is supplied here because the cited edition itself has not yet been available for direct page verification.

Chapter Fifteen

The Modern State Is Not the Classical Imamate

The preceding chapters have examined theft, ḥirāba, zinā, qadhf, drinking, rebellion, and apostasy through Aḥmad Fatḥī Bahnasi's account. Each offense reveals disagreement over definition, evidence, legal status, procedure, and punishment. Beneath those disputes lies a larger institutional question: who is the authority expected to enforce these rules?[162]

Classical jurists wrote within a political world organized around the imam, caliph, sultan, judge, local governor, religious community, and differentiated legal status. The modern state is built differently. It possesses centralized bureaucracy, permanent police forces, prisons, intelligence services, forensic laboratories, national identity systems, mass surveillance, written constitutions, legislatures, political parties, and administrative agencies. Its power over territory, citizenship, communication, education, documentation, and personal identity is more integrated than anything available to a classical ruler.

The question is not whether a modern government can reproduce the outward form of a classical punishment. It plainly can. The real question is:

> *Does a modern government inherit the religious authority assumed within classical doctrine merely because it possesses the physical power to enforce it?*

The answer advanced here is no.

---

162 Aḥmad Fatḥī Bahnasi, Al-Ḥudūd fī al-Islām, Shuʿāʿ al-Islām no. 12 (Alexandria: Muʾassasat Shabāb al-Jāmiʿa, n.d.), 30–39, 61–90, 99–159, together with the work's sections on ḥirāba, zinā, al-baghy, and apostasy. Across these discussions, enforcement is assigned to the imam, ruler, or judge rather than to private individuals.

The Institutional Assumption Beneath the Ḥudūd

Bahnasi repeatedly speaks of the imam, ruler, or judge as the authority that receives complaints, evaluates proof, prevents private vengeance, orders punishment, and protects public order. The model presumes a political authority located within an Islamic legal and moral structure and expected to recognize jurists, appoint judges, administer religiously informed law, and enforce rights classified as belonging to God or individuals.[163]

That structure cannot be transferred automatically into the contemporary nation-state. A modern president is one officer within a constitutional system, usually limited by legislation, courts, elections, terms of office, and divided governmental powers. A president does not become an imam by adopting the title. A monarch does not become a caliph by invoking religion. A military ruler does not acquire sacred authority through control of the army.

Territorial Citizenship Is Not Religious Membership

The modern state is organized through borders, nationality, passports, residence, citizenship, and international recognition. Its population may include Muslims, Christians, Jews, adherents of other religions, former believers, and persons without religious affiliation. Its authority is territorial rather than purely confessional.

Citizenship should remain stable despite conversion, disbelief, denominational change, criticism of religion, or refusal to identify religiously. The classical fusion of religious and political membership cannot be preserved without making citizenship unequal and conditional. A modern citizen does not leave the state by leaving a religion.

Centralized Coercion and the Magnification of Error

The modern state claims a monopoly over legitimate force through police, military, prosecution, courts, prisons, and official punishment.

---

163 Bahnasi, Al-Ḥudūd fī al-Islām, 30–39, 61–90, 99–159, together with the sections on ḥirāba, zinā, al-baghy, and apostasy, for judicial authority, proof, punishment, and the distinction between the rights of God and individuals.

When such an institution sacralizes its criminal law, it combines divine language with unprecedented coercive capacity. That combination is exceptionally dangerous.[164]

A mistaken rule in a centralized system can be applied nationally. A legislature may define apostasy broadly; a ministry may circulate one interpretation to every court; a national database may identify suspects; and state media may publicize punishment. Centralization magnifies both administrative efficiency and human error.

Punishment is also distributed across institutions. Investigators, forensic specialists, prosecutors, religious consultants, judges, appellate courts, prison officials, medical personnel, and executioners each perform one part of the process. This diffusion can obscure responsibility. The final injury emerges from the machinery as a whole, while each actor claims to have performed only a limited task.

Codification Converts Juristic Plurality into State Command

Classical jurisprudence preserved multiple schools, disputed opinions, exceptions, and flexible interpretive practices. The modern state prefers codification. A statute must tell police, prosecutors, and judges what rule applies. Government must therefore select among juristic opinions.[165]

For theft, it must choose the threshold, protected custody, treatment of public property, and repeated offenses. For zinā, it must choose the conditions of iḥṣān, the evidentiary structure, confession, retraction, and stoning. For drinking, it must choose the meaning of khamr and forty or eighty lashes. For apostasy, it must define departure, waiting periods, repentance, and the treatment of women.

Selection is legislation. Once government chooses one opinion and excludes others, it cannot truthfully claim that it merely implemented a

164Wael B. Hallaq, The Impossible State: Islam, Politics, and Modernity's Moral Predicament (New York: Columbia University Press, 2013), especially the analysis of the structural difference between the modern sovereign state and premodern Islamic governance.

165Wael B. Hallaq, Shari'a: Theory, Practice, Transformations (Cambridge: Cambridge University Press, 2009), on juristic plurality and the transformation produced by modern state codification.

complete and self-executing divine code. It has decided which school governs, which minority positions disappear, how historical rules are translated, and how gaps are filled.

The state may also create a hybrid code by combining one school's definition, another school's evidence, a third school's punishment, and modern police procedure. Such a code may never have existed in the classical tradition, yet it may still be presented rhetorically as God's law.

Political Legislation Protected by Sacred Language

In a representative system, legislation is produced through human institutions. Legislators debate, committees amend, courts interpret, and political parties bargain. A ḥadd statute may be supported from sincere religious conviction, electoral advantage, coalition pressure, or public fear. Its political origin cannot be erased by attaching sacred language to the final text.

An ordinary statute can be criticized, reviewed, and amended. A sacralized statute may be treated as untouchable. Opponents are accused of resisting religion rather than questioning legislation. The law becomes human in creation but rhetorically divine in protection.

Constitutional Supremacy and Judicial Independence

A modern constitutional order places all public power under a higher legal framework protecting life, bodily integrity, equality, due process, religious freedom, expression, and judicial review. No ordinary statute should escape those limits. If a religiously framed punishment is placed above the constitution, constitutional government collapses.[166]

The ruler cannot be simultaneously limited and sacred. Constitutional office exists because public authority is fallible and reviewable. Sacred immunity denies that premise.

Judicial independence is especially vulnerable in cases involving apostasy, rebellion, public morality, or religious insult. Judges may face pressure from executives, security agencies, official religious institutions, and public outrage. When government appoints the

---

166International Covenant on Civil and Political Rights, arts. 2, 6, 7, 14, 18, 19, and 26, 999 U.N.T.S. 171.

religious experts whose opinions define orthodoxy, theology becomes part of political administration.

Authoritarian Capture and Symbolic Legitimacy

Formal constitutions and courts do not prevent authoritarian capture. A ruler may use religious criminal law to silence opponents, regulate private life, justify emergency power, and display moral authority. Public enforcement of the ḥudūd may become symbolic proof that a politically insecure regime is authentically Islamic.

The body of the convicted person then becomes an instrument of legitimacy. Amputation, flogging, stoning, or execution may be performed not because the specific harm requires it, but because visible punishment communicates strength, piety, independence, or resistance to foreign influence.

A person's body should not bear the cost of a civilization's identity crisis. Historical injury, colonial disruption, or cultural humiliation cannot justify present mutilation and execution.

The Modern Police State and the Collapse of Historical Privacy Barriers

Classical rules often depended upon conduct becoming public through witnesses, complaint, or confession. The modern state can discover private life through electronic surveillance, phone records, cameras, informants, digital searches, biometric systems, hotel records, and data analysis.[167]

This changes the practical meaning of the law. The four-witness rule once made private zinā extremely difficult to prove. Modern authorities may attempt to substitute video, forensic evidence, location data, or private messages. Technology does not merely improve proof; it expands the state's capacity to criminalize private relationships, conversion, association, intoxication, and dissent.

A rule that was rarely enforceable in a low-surveillance environment may become systematically enforceable under a modern security

---

167 Bahnasi, Al-Ḥudūd fī al-Islām, section on zinā, especially the evidentiary discussions concerning confession, witnesses, and judicial proof; see also Gabriel, "Reforming Hudud Ordinances," 98–100, on the classical evidentiary structure.

apparatus. The modern state is therefore not a neutral vessel carrying an old rule. It transforms the rule by increasing the state's ability to reach the person.

Modern Evidence Requires New Legislation

Scientific evidence may improve accuracy, but it also creates questions the classical categories do not answer. Should DNA establish zinā? Should toxicology prove drinking? Should digital records prove apostasy? Should facial recognition identify a participant in rebellion? Government must legislate anew.

Modern knowledge may also challenge earlier assumptions regarding intoxication, pregnancy, coercion, mental illness, and bodily capacity for punishment. A state cannot invoke classical authority while ignoring contemporary scientific knowledge whenever that knowledge complicates enforcement.

Human Rights and the Citizen's Claim Against the State

The modern state exists within an international legal order. It may voluntarily accept obligations concerning life, torture, cruel punishment, equality, fair trial, and religious freedom. The issue is not whether international law replaces religion, but whether government may violate dignity after undertaking legal obligations to protect it.[168]

Modern constitutionalism also transforms the subject into a citizen possessing enforceable claims against government. The citizen may challenge unlawful arrest, discriminatory law, censorship, torture, and arbitrary punishment. Criminal responsibility should not depend upon religion, freedom status, sex, inherited identity, or theological classification.

The Ideal State Objection

Defenders of the ḥudūd sometimes argue that these punishments should be enforced only after an ideal government establishes justice, welfare, equality, piety, and judicial independence. The intuition that social justice must precede severe punishment has moral force. A government

---

168International Covenant on Civil and Political Rights, arts. 6, 7, 14, 18, and 26.

that tolerates hunger and corruption should not mutilate a person for survival theft.

But no level of welfare makes mutilation necessary, and no ideal state exists. Human governments remain fallible. A legal theory whose justice depends upon perfect rulers, perfect courts, truthful witnesses, and incorruptible police is unsuitable for actual law.

Constitutional institutions must be designed for bad rulers as well as good ones. The more severe and irreversible the punishment, the less acceptable it is to rely upon idealized authority. The state most capable of enforcing the ḥudūd efficiently is also the state whose power requires the greatest restraint.

Continuity, Colonialism, and Symbolic Restoration

Restorationists may describe modern enforcement as continuity with an Islamic legal obligation interrupted by colonialism or secularization. Colonial transformation is historically real, but institutional continuity cannot be assumed where sovereignty, citizenship, bureaucracy, policing, and surveillance have changed fundamentally.[169]

The modern state is not the classical polity with electricity, ministries, and passports. Its structure is different, its coercive reach is broader, and its relationship to the citizen is constitutionally transformed. The proper response to historical injury is not romantic repetition, but responsible construction of justice within present institutions.

No Institution May Displace Its Moral Responsibility

The ruler may claim that the punishment belongs to God and that no human discretion remains. Yet discretion has already been exercised through selection of the juristic opinion, enactment of the statute, appointment of officials, definition of evidence, and ordering of enforcement.

The judge may say that his duty is only to apply the law. The executioner may say that he merely obeyed an order. This chain of displaced responsibility permits everyone to participate while no one

---

169Hallaq, The Impossible State, on the discontinuity between the modern state and the moral-legal structure of premodern Islamic governance.

accepts moral agency. A constitutional order must reject that disappearance of responsibility.

No modern official can prove divine delegation for a specific code selected from disputed jurisprudence. Government may punish humanly identifiable harms and regulate public conduct. It cannot establish that it acts directly on behalf of God.

Religious Moral Authority Without Penal Sacralization

Religion may shape public ethics without becoming a penal ministry. Islamic teaching can contribute principles of justice, honesty, family responsibility, care for the poor, protection of life, and restraint of power. Those values may inform legislation. Informing law is not the same as sacralizing punishment.

A Muslim-majority state may remain ethically informed by Islam while organizing criminal law around equal citizenship, legality, harm, consent, culpability, proportionality, bodily integrity, freedom of conscience, independent courts, and reviewable sanctions.

Religious institutions may teach, advise, counsel, publish, and participate in democratic debate. Their influence should operate through persuasion, not authority to order execution, amputation, or compelled belief. Classical jurisprudence remains valuable as intellectual history, moral reasoning, and sustained engagement with justice, but it need not be transplanted directly into a modern penal code.[170]

The True Responsibility of Modern Institutions

A legislature cannot escape responsibility by citing earlier jurists. It must ask what law is just now in light of present institutions, scientific knowledge, constitutional rights, social conditions, and foreseeable abuse. A court must protect individuals against political pressure, theological accusation, coerced confession, unequal evidence, and irreversible punishment.

The moral character of a state is not proved by the severity of its punishments. It is proved by protection of the weak, fairness of courts, honesty of government, restraint of power, and respect for dignity. A

170Mohammad Hashim Kamali, Shariah Law: An Introduction (Oxford: Oneworld, 2008); Hallaq, Shari'a: Theory, Practice, Transformations.

state that amputates thieves while tolerating official corruption has not established justice. A state that punishes private morality while permitting public oppression has not established morality. A state that kills apostates while silencing truth has not protected faith.

Conclusion

The restorationist project assumes that the modern state can inherit the authority of the classical imamate. Yet the modern state is more centralized, intrusive, bureaucratic, technologically powerful, and constitutionally different. The classical law it seeks to restore is juristically plural, historically situated, procedurally cautious, and dependent upon status categories that cannot be accepted within equal citizenship.

The contradiction is stark:

> *The institution most capable of enforcing the ḥudūd is also the institution least entitled to treat its own coercive choices as divine.*

The distinction must remain explicit. A modern president is not automatically an imam. A legislature does not become a council of jurists merely by citing them. Police do not acquire religious authority through uniforms, and judges do not administer divine judgment because a statute uses sacred language.

Every punishment remains a human act performed by human institutions upon human bodies. Government must accept full responsibility for every rule it enacts and every injury it causes. The foundational conclusion is therefore:

> *A modern government may draw ethical insight from Islamic tradition, but it may not inherit sacred immunity for its coercive power.*

The next chapter turns directly to the evolution of this study's argument, from procedural reform toward the conclusion that procedural reform alone cannot resolve the underlying problem.

Chapter Sixteen

Why Procedural Reform Is No Longer Sufficient

The argument developed in this study did not begin with the conclusion that the classical ḥudūd should be removed from the lawful authority of the modern state. It began from a more limited reformist position. That earlier position sought to preserve the punishments while reducing injustice through constitutional supremacy, strict legality, independent courts, presumption of innocence, proof beyond reasonable doubt, rejection of coerced confession, appellate review, equal treatment, and careful attention to necessity and social conditions.[171]

That approach was not without value. It recognized the danger of allowing governments to invoke Islamic criminal law without constitutional restraint. It drew attention to humane doctrines already present within the juristic tradition and attempted to reinforce them through contemporary institutions. Yet the detailed examination of Bahnasi's work leads beyond that earlier position. The problem is not only that severe punishments may be imposed through defective procedures. The punishments themselves are often disproportionate, irreversible, unequal, or directed toward conduct that should not fall within criminal authority at all.

> *This is why procedural reform is no longer sufficient.*

The Earlier Reformist Hope

The reformist project rested upon a plausible intuition. Classical law contains demanding evidentiary rules, doctrines of doubt, restrictions upon confession, defenses of necessity and coercion, reluctance toward public exposure, and repeated efforts to avert the fixed punishments. It

171Mark A. Gabriel, 'Reforming Hudud Ordinances to Reconcile Islamic Criminal Law with International Human Rights Law' (PhD diss., University of Cape Town, 2016), especially the constitutional and procedural reform framework developed throughout the dissertation.

therefore seemed possible that stronger constitutional safeguards might reconcile the ḥudūd with modern human-rights obligations.[172]

Under this approach, the deepest danger appeared to arise from abusive implementation rather than from the penalties themselves. Better courts, more reliable evidence, and stronger review were expected to discipline enforcement. These protections remain essential to every legitimate criminal system. But they answer only part of the legal question.

A Fair Procedure Can Enforce an Unjust Law

Procedure determines how government reaches judgment. It asks whether the law was published, whether the accused was properly charged, whether evidence was reliable, whether confession was voluntary, whether counsel was available, whether the judge was impartial, and whether appeal was permitted. These questions are indispensable. They do not determine whether the underlying offense or punishment is just.

A person may receive competent counsel, an independent judge, full access to evidence, an open trial, and appellate review. If the state then executes that person for peacefully changing religion, the process may be formally fair while the result remains unjust. A court may establish private consensual zinā beyond doubt, yet stoning remains illegitimate. Theft may be proven accurately, yet amputation remains irreversible and disproportionate. The quality of the trial cannot transform the nature of the punishment.[173]

---

172 Aḥmad Fatḥī Bahnasi, Al-Ḥudūd fī al-Islām, Shuʿāʿ al-Islām no. 12 (Alexandria: Muʾassasat Shabāb al-Jāmiʿa, n.d.), 61–90, 99–159, together with the sections on ḥirāba, zinā, al-baghy, and apostasy, for doubt, confession, testimony, necessity, coercion, and barriers to fixed punishment; see also Gabriel, "Reforming Hudud Ordinances," 98–100, 160–97.

173For the distinction between fair procedure and substantive injustice, see International Covenant on Civil and Political Rights, arts. 6, 7, 17, 18, and 26; Gabriel, 'Reforming Hudud Ordinances,' chapters 5–7.

Procedure Cannot Legitimize an Illegitimate Offense

Apostasy provides the clearest example. The problem is not primarily insufficient evidence, coerced confession, or judicial bias. The deeper problem is that government lacks legitimate authority to punish peaceful religious change. Even perfect proof cannot cure an illegitimate offense.

The same principle applies to private consensual sexual conduct. The state may prove the act with certainty. That certainty does not create a public injury warranting flogging or death. The legal question is not merely whether the conduct occurred, but whether the state should punish it bodily at all.

Procedure Cannot Make Mutilation Proportionate

In theft, the court may establish ownership, protected custody, minimum value, voluntary taking, and absence of legally recognized doubt. Yet the sentence still removes a functioning part of the body permanently. Accuracy and proportionality are separate questions. The most reliable conviction does not make mutilation proportionate.

The same is true of cross-amputation, stoning, crucifixion, and execution. Every trial remains vulnerable to false testimony, forged documents, mistaken interpretation, scientific development, recantation, or new evidence. Procedural perfection is an illusion; irreversibility is real. A legal order committed to institutional humility should avoid punishments that no later justice can undo.[174]

The Doctrine of Doubt Is Valuable but Insufficient

The instruction to avert the ḥudūd in cases of doubt is one of the most humane principles in the classical tradition. It should be preserved as a broad rule of criminal restraint. But it cannot answer the case in which no legally recognized doubt remains. The doctrine asks whether the

---

174 Gabriel, "Reforming Hudud Ordinances," 176–99, on corporal and capital punishments and proposed alternatives; see also Bahnasi, Al-Ḥudūd fī al-Islām, 61–90 and the sections on ḥirāba, zinā, and apostasy.

offense has been established. It does not ask whether the punishment is compatible with dignity.[175]

Doubt also depends upon human interpretation. One school may recognize an ambiguity another rejects. One judge may regard a marriage as defective and therefore protective; another may classify it differently. One court may accept a claim of ownership or entitlement; another may dismiss it. The principle reduces harm, but it cannot eliminate inconsistency.

High Evidentiary Thresholds Do Not Justify Severe Punishment

A common defense of the ḥudūd is that they are rarely enforceable because proof is exceptionally difficult. Rarity may reduce the number of injuries. It does not establish the legitimacy of the punishment. An unjust sentence does not become just because it is seldom imposed.

The classical structure often places mercy before conviction rather than within sentencing. Before proof is complete, concealment, retraction, doubt, pardon, repentance, or reconciliation may prevent the ḥadd. After technical completion, discretion narrows. Mercy therefore becomes dependent upon evidentiary accident, timing, or school-specific classification rather than an open judgment about proportionality.

Mercy Should Not Depend upon Technical Escape

Two persons may commit the same act. One case contains a technical ambiguity, and the ḥadd falls. The other contains no recognized ambiguity, and the full bodily punishment follows. The difference may not reflect greater harm or culpability. It may arise from available language, the timing of confession, witness agreement, or the governing school.

A humane system should be able to consider motive, necessity, remorse, restitution, vulnerability, prior history, rehabilitation, and social context openly. It should not force the judge to search for a

---

175 Bahnasi, Al-Ḥudūd fī al-Islām, 61–90, 99–159, together with the sections on ḥirāba and zinā, for the recurring use of shubha and procedural barriers; see also Gabriel, "Reforming Hudud Ordinances," 98–100, 160–97.

technical defect in order to avoid an unjust result. Where compassion must hide inside procedural doubt, the substantive law has become too rigid.

Severe Punishment Distorts Procedure

Bahnasi's own account shows that the punishment shapes the procedure surrounding it. The severity of stoning shapes reluctance toward confession. Amputation shapes the development of ownership doubts and protected-custody requirements. The danger of flogging shapes witness rules, concealment, and retraction. Procedure is not independent of the endpoint; it is constructed around fear of what follows.[176]

This can produce humane avoidance, but also instability. One judge finds doubt; another refuses it. One government suspends enforcement; another uses it symbolically. Justice then depends upon interpretive creativity rather than transparent principle. A legal order should not require inconsistency in order to remain humane.

Procedural Reform Cannot Cure Unequal Personhood

The classical penal structure distributes protection and responsibility according to freedom, religion, sex, chastity, marital history, sanity, and age. Equal procedure applied to unequal substantive law remains unequal. Reforming courtroom process cannot cure status-based rules unless those rules themselves are changed.

A modern legal order must provide equal protection for Muslims and non-Muslims, equal testimonial evaluation for men and women, universal protection of reputation, and full dignity regardless of prior sexual history, disability, birth, or inherited status. These changes are necessary, but they substantially revise the classical structure. Once substantive revision is accepted for equality, there is no principled reason to declare corporal punishment itself untouchable.

---

176 Bahnasi, Al-Ḥudūd fī al-Islām, 61–90, 99–159, together with the section on zinā, for confession and retraction, ownership and ḥirz, witness requirements, and evidentiary disagreement; see also Gabriel, "Reforming Hudud Ordinances," 95–101, 124–26.

Selective Immutability

Some restorationist projects permit change in procedure, evidence, institutions, codification, technology, status rules, and administration while resisting change at the point of bodily punishment. Everything surrounding the sentence may be modernized, but the sentence alone is declared fixed.

This is selective immutability. It allows a modern legislature to choose among schools, define new evidentiary rules, abolish slavery-based distinctions, and employ contemporary police methods, yet treats amputation, flogging, stoning, or execution as beyond reconsideration. Such selectivity requires stronger justification than tradition alone.

Human Rights Are Substantive as Well as Procedural

Human rights protect not only fair trial but life, bodily integrity, equality, privacy, conscience, expression, and freedom from cruel punishment. A trial may satisfy procedural rights while violating these substantive protections. Bodily integrity cannot be reduced to accuracy of conviction; freedom of conscience cannot be reduced to fairness of an apostasy hearing; and privacy cannot be reduced to reliability of evidence concerning private conduct.[177]

Formal equality is also insufficient. A law may apply the same corporal punishment to every citizen and still remain cruel and disproportionate. Equal exposure to mutilation is not equal justice.

The Earlier Reformist Position Underestimated the Modern State

The earlier reformist position assumed that modern institutions could restrain the punishments. The preceding chapter showed the reverse danger. The modern state possesses surveillance, digital evidence, centralized databases, forensic testing, national police forces, and bureaucratic systems capable of making enforcement more invasive and systematic than in the classical period.

Traditional procedural barriers developed in a low-surveillance environment. Video, private messages, location data, toxicology, and

---

177International Covenant on Civil and Political Rights, arts. 6, 7, 17, 18, 19, and 26.

biometric identification may expose conduct that once remained hidden. Procedural modernization can therefore make punishments more reachable rather than less.

Nor can technical safeguards reliably control authoritarian institutions. A constitution may promise due process while government controls police, prosecutors, courts, religious institutions, and media. The danger is greatest in cases involving rebellion, apostasy, dissent, and public morality.

From Reforming Enforcement to Questioning Authority

The progression of the argument can be stated simply. The first question was: how can the ḥudūd be enforced more fairly? The deeper question became: should the modern state enforce these punishments at all?

This shift is not an abandonment of scholarship. It results from taking the evidence more seriously. Bahnasi seeks to explain and defend Islamic criminal law, yet his detailed account reveals juristic disagreement, historical variation, dependence upon custom, unequal status, procedural avoidance, and discretionary construction. The more closely the rules are examined, the harder it becomes to treat the punishments as one simple divine command awaiting implementation.[178]

For every major offense, the state must choose definitions, conditions, evidence, exceptions, status rules, and procedure. The punishment becomes operative only after human institutions construct the offense. Human construction combined with irreversible punishment is the central danger.

Moral Purpose and Penal Form Must Be Distinguished

The reformist position often assumed that rejecting a punishment meant rejecting the moral value associated with it. That assumption is false. Theft can remain wrong without amputation. Armed violence can remain grave without crucifixion. Adultery can remain morally

---

178 Bahnasi, Al-Ḥudūd fī al-Islām, 30–39, 61–90, 99–159, together with the sections on ḥirāba, zinā, al-baghy, and apostasy; Wael B. Hallaq, Shariʿa: Theory, Practice, Transformations (Cambridge: Cambridge University Press, 2009), on juristic plurality and the historical structure of Islamic law.

condemned without stoning. False accusation can remain punishable without flogging. Intoxication can remain religiously prohibited without corporal enforcement. Apostasy can remain theologically serious without criminalization.

The law should preserve property, life, public security, family responsibility, reputation, reason, and social peace. It need not preserve every historical punishment attached to those interests. If the purposes are justice, protection, mercy, and prevention of harm, the means must be judged by whether they serve those ends. The instrument cannot become more sacred than the purpose.

When Reform Must Become Replacement

A project may narrow proof, delay enforcement, add appeals, regulate instruments, or require medical supervision. These measures reduce harm. But medical supervision does not make amputation morally legitimate, regulated flogging remains deliberate pain, and a longer apostasy trial remains prosecution of conscience.

Where the wrong lies in the offense itself, the method of punishment, or the authority claimed by government, reform must move beyond adjustment. The institution must be replaced. This study does not reject every principle of classical criminal reasoning. It preserves necessity, coercion, restraint, restitution, reconciliation, individual responsibility, and protection of victims while rejecting mutilation, public corporal punishment, stoning, crucifixion, religious execution, and unequal personhood.

The Scholar's Responsibility to Move Beyond an Earlier Position

A scholar should not preserve an earlier conclusion merely for consistency. Where deeper study shows that a framework is insufficient, intellectual honesty requires change. The movement beyond procedural reform is therefore not an embarrassment; it is the result of sustained engagement.

Gabriel's earlier doctoral project sought reconciliation between Islamic criminal law and international human-rights law through constitutional safeguards and restricted enforcement. That work remains important because it identified the danger of arbitrary state action and emphasized due process. The present study reaches a more demanding conclusion: some conflicts cannot be reconciled by procedure alone. Where government claims authority to mutilate, kill for private morality, punish conversion, or distribute dignity unequally, the conflict is substantive.[179]

The state must relinquish certain powers. That is not the failure of reform. It is the completion of reform's logic.

A Transformed Substantive System

Rejecting the classical punishments does not leave government powerless. It may use restitution, compensation, proportionate detention, supervision, rehabilitation, treatment, civil remedies, protective orders, and precise laws against violence, coercion, exploitation, and serious fraud. These responses can be reviewed, adjusted, and corrected.

Modern punishment should preserve the possibility of appeal, reconsideration, release, rehabilitation, and compensation. Where public protection can be achieved through a less irreversible measure, the state should choose it. This principle of least irreversible coercion does not prohibit serious punishment. It prohibits unnecessary destruction.

Criminal law should focus upon conduct causing or threatening substantial harm. It should punish violence, theft, coercion, exploitation, serious fraud, and public danger. It should not punish peaceful belief, religious departure, private identity, or inherited status. Justice should restore victims and prevent recurrence before it displays power upon the body.

179Gabriel, 'Reforming Hudud Ordinances,' especially the proposed reconciliation through constitutional safeguards and human-rights limitations. The present argument marks a further development beyond that earlier position.

Conclusion

Procedural reform was an important beginning. It recognized the danger of arbitrary government and the need to restrain punishment through legality, reliable evidence, judicial independence, and constitutional protection. But Bahnasi's work reveals that the conflict reaches beyond procedure. The offenses are constructed through disputed human judgment; the punishments are frequently irreversible; legal personhood is unequally defined; state authority is sacralized; and private morality and conscience are criminalized.

The governing principle is:

> *Procedural reform is necessary wherever criminal law operates, but it is insufficient where the offense itself is illegitimate or the punishment itself violates dignity.*

From that principle follows the larger conclusion:

> *The ḥudūd cannot be reconciled with the modern constitutional state merely by making enforcement more careful. The corporal, capital, political, and conscience-based punishments themselves must be removed from the state's lawful authority.*

The moral purposes associated with them need not be abandoned. They must be preserved through different institutions, different penalties, and a different understanding of justice. The next chapter develops that constructive alternative.

Chapter Seventeen

Preserving Moral Purposes Without Preserving the Punishments

The argument of this study does not end with rejection. To conclude only that amputation, flogging, stoning, crucifixion, execution for apostasy, and sacralized punishment should be removed from the authority of the modern state would leave the work incomplete. The deeper task is constructive. What moral concerns did the classical ḥudūd seek to protect? Which of those concerns remain legitimate? How may they be preserved without preserving the punishments historically attached to them?[180]

The classical jurists did not construct the ḥudūd as random acts of cruelty. They believed they were protecting essential interests: property, life, public security, family integrity, reputation, reason, political order, and religious community. The problem is not that these concerns are meaningless. The problem is that the punishments developed around them are no longer acceptable methods through which a modern state should pursue them.

> *The moral purposes associated with the ḥudūd can be preserved more faithfully by abandoning the punishments than by preserving them.*

Purpose and Instrument

A legal tradition must distinguish between an objective and the means historically used to pursue it. The objective may endure while the instrument does not. A society may continue to value honesty, fidelity, sobriety, public safety, family responsibility, and religious seriousness without reproducing every historical penalty once associated with those values.

---

180 Aḥmad Fatḥī Bahnasi, Al-Ḥudūd fī al-Islām, Shuʿāʿ al-Islām no. 12 (Alexandria: Muʾassasat Shabāb al-Jāmiʿa, n.d.); Mark A. Gabriel, "Reforming Hudud Ordinances to Reconcile Islamic Criminal Law with International Human Rights Law" (PhD diss., University of Cape Town, 2016), especially 93–126, 160–99.

The means may eventually become more sacred than the ends. Amputation comes to symbolize protection of property; stoning, family morality; flogging, honor or sobriety; and execution for apostasy, defense of faith. Yet symbolic association does not prove that the punishment continues to serve the purpose. If amputation creates poverty and dependence, if stoning transforms private morality into public violence, if flogging fails to restore reputation, or if apostasy law produces hypocrisy, the historical instrument has begun to defeat the moral objective.[181]

The Principle of Moral Translation

The task is not mechanical preservation but moral translation. Moral translation asks what human good a rule sought to protect, what harm it attempted to prevent, what modern institution can serve that purpose more justly, what safeguards are required against abuse, and what remains a matter of religion rather than state coercion. This approach preserves seriousness without freezing history.

Protecting Property Without Amputation

The law of theft expresses a valid purpose: property should be secure, unlawful taking should be restrained, and victims should receive justice. Property supports personal independence, family stability, commerce, trust, and social order. Rejecting amputation therefore does not weaken the protection of property. It reconstructs that protection around proportionality, restitution, and repair.[182]

The victim ordinarily needs stolen property returned or the loss compensated. Modern law should prioritize restitution, recovery of assets, compensation, and repair. It should distinguish survival theft, opportunistic theft, repeated professional theft, breach of trust,

---

181 Bahnasi, Al-Ḥudūd fī al-Islām, 30–39, 61–90, 99–159, together with the sections on ḥirāba, zinā, al-baghy, and apostasy; Wael B. Hallaq, Shariʿa: Theory, Practice, Transformations (Cambridge: Cambridge University Press, 2009).

182 Bahnasi, Al-Ḥudūd fī al-Islām, 61–90, on theft, its conditions, protected custody, thresholds, and amputation; Gabriel, "Reforming Hudud Ordinances," 193–94, 198–99, on proportionality and alternatives to corporal punishment.

organized theft, cybertheft, violent robbery, and public corruption. Sentence and remedy should reflect value, planning, motive, harm, restitution, and prior conduct.

A serious property system must also address the unequal visibility of wrongdoing. Petty theft is easily seen, while embezzlement, procurement fraud, diversion of public funds, and organized financial crime may cause far greater social injury. The moral purpose of protecting wealth is not fulfilled when the poor are punished visibly and the powerful remain beyond effective law.

Protecting Public Security Without Spectacle

Classical jurists developed the doctrine of ḥirāba in part to protect roads, travelers, life, property, and public peace against organized violence. Modern societies face armed robbery, kidnapping, terrorism, gang violence, attacks upon transportation, and organized intimidation. Government must respond firmly, but firmness does not require crucifixion or cross-amputation.

The law should define actual conduct: murder, attempted murder, armed robbery, kidnapping, terrorism, hostage-taking, extortion, and organized violent conspiracy. Each offense should require proof of conduct, intention, individual participation, and harm. Where offenders remain dangerous, secure detention may be necessary, but incapacitation should not become mutilation or public display.

The classical effect given to repentance before capture contains a useful practical insight. Modern law may encourage offenders to cease violence, release victims, surrender weapons, return property, and cooperate with authorities through proportionate mitigation, while preserving accountability for grave crimes and the rights of victims.[183]

Protecting Family Integrity Through Consent and Responsibility

Classical jurists associated the law of zinā with the protection of marriage, lineage, fidelity, family responsibility, and social morality. Those concerns should not be dismissed. Adultery can cause serious

183 Bahnasi, Al-Ḥudūd fī al-Islām, section on ḥirāba and the effect of repentance before capture; Gabriel, "Reforming Hudud Ordinances," 196–99.

emotional and financial harm, and sexual exploitation can devastate families. Yet government must distinguish moral betrayal from violence and coercion.

Modern sexual criminal law should be organized around consent and vulnerability. It should punish rape, sexual assault, child abuse, trafficking, exploitation, coercion, abuse of authority, and nonconsensual recording. These offenses involve identifiable injury and require serious public response.

Consensual adultery may remain a grave moral wrong and a breach of marital trust. Its consequences may be addressed through divorce, financial remedies, parental responsibility, protection against disease transmission, and custody decisions directed toward the welfare of children. The state does not need to flog or stone in order to recognize betrayal. Family integrity is strengthened more effectively through counseling, protection from abuse, child-support enforcement, and social services than through policing bedrooms.

Protecting Reputation Through Repair

The classical law of qadhf sought to prevent sexual slander and protect honor. This remains one of its strongest moral purposes. False accusation can destroy family relationships, employment, public standing, and psychological well-being. Modern law should protect reputation seriously, equally, and restoratively.[184]

Protection should not depend upon religion, sex, freedom status, chastity, disability, or social rank. Remedies may include correction, retraction, apology, compensation, removal of defamatory material, injunctions against repetition, and narrowly defined criminal penalties for deliberate and grave falsehood. These measures serve the injured person more directly than flogging the speaker.

The law must also protect good-faith reporting of rape, child abuse, professional misconduct, and other wrongdoing. A person seeking medical care, legal advice, or public accountability should not face punishment merely because four eyewitnesses cannot be produced.

184Bahnasi, Al-Ḥudūd fī al-Islām, 99–139, on qadhf, protection of reputation, evidentiary requirements, and punishment.

Protecting Reason Through Public Health

The prohibition of intoxicants seeks to preserve reason, self-control, family welfare, prayer, and public safety. Alcohol and other substances may contribute to addiction, violence, traffic deaths, neglect, and medical harm. These are legitimate public concerns, but punishment should be directed toward actual harm and risk rather than private religious nonconformity.

A modern framework may use age restrictions, licensing, impaired-driving laws, workplace safety rules, treatment programs, warning requirements, regulation of dangerous distribution, and intervention in abuse or neglect. Where dependence exists, medical care, counseling, rehabilitation, and family support are more rational than flogging. Pain does not cure addiction.[185]

Muslims may continue to regard complete abstinence as a binding religious duty, and religious institutions may teach that duty clearly. Moral teaching and civil regulation can coexist without becoming identical.

Protecting Political Order Without Sacralizing Rulers

Classical jurists understood baghy as a doctrine concerned with civil conflict, political unity, and the limitation of bloodshed. Those aims remain vital, but political order should be constitutional rather than sacredly attached to one ruler. Elections, criticism, journalism, protest, civil disobedience, and political organization must remain protected. Peaceful challenge is not rebellion; it is part of legitimate political life.

Where organized violence occurs, government may respond, but force must be necessary, proportionate, individually directed, and subject to independent review. The classical restraints toward prisoners, wounded persons, families, and property should be preserved. After violence ends, reconciliation should seek truth, accountability, compensation, reintegration, and prevention of renewed conflict. Victory should not become revenge.

---

185 Bahnasi, Al-Ḥudūd fī al-Islām, 145–59, on intoxicants and corporal punishment; Gabriel, "Reforming Hudud Ordinances," 180–83, 198–99, on alcohol and alternative sanctions.

Protecting Religion Through Freedom

Classical apostasy doctrine was commonly justified in terms of protecting religious community, loyalty, and faith. Yet faith cannot be protected through coercion without changing its nature. A person compelled to remain Muslim outwardly does not thereby become faithful inwardly. Religion is preserved more authentically through teaching, persuasion, moral credibility, example, and freedom.[186]

The state may protect houses of worship, religious education, peaceful preaching, and believers against discrimination or violence. It may punish coercive conversion and attacks upon religious communities. It should not punish peaceful departure. Where a person commits espionage, armed collaboration, or violence, the conduct may be prosecuted independently. Religious change itself should remain protected.

Dignity, Accountability, and the Victim

Across every offense, one moral objective should govern reconstruction: human dignity. Dignity belongs to the victim, the accused, the convicted offender, the dissenter, the believer, and the nonbeliever. It does not disappear after wrongdoing.

Respect for dignity does not mean absence of punishment. A person may be convicted, imprisoned, restrained, fined, supervised, or required to compensate victims. But punishment should not deny that the offender remains human. Reform must also avoid becoming so offender-centered that victims disappear. Victims need recognition, safety, restitution, compensation, participation, and access to justice.

Where appropriate, restorative approaches may bring together acknowledgment of wrongdoing, victim needs, offender responsibility, compensation, and community repair. Not every offense permits direct reconciliation, but the principle of repair should influence sentencing broadly. Rehabilitation should preserve the possibility that a person can change through education, treatment, employment support, and supervised reintegration.

---

186 Bahnasi, Al-Ḥudūd fī al-Islām, apostasy section, on apostasy and repentance; Gabriel, "Reforming Hudud Ordinances," 110–12, 176–80; International Covenant on Civil and Political Rights, arts. 18 and 19.

The Maqāṣid as Living Purposes

The higher purposes of law should not be invoked merely to defend inherited punishments. They should be allowed to evaluate those punishments. If the aims include preservation of life, intellect, property, family, religion, and dignity, the means should not destroy those same goods unnecessarily.[187]

Stoning, crucifixion, and execution for peaceful apostasy destroy life where no violent threat requires it. Flogging the addicted person does not necessarily restore reason. Amputation may diminish the capacity for work and restitution. Killing or mutilating a parent may devastate children and dependents. Compelled belief produces fear rather than faith. Public humiliation and bodily spectacle directly assault dignity.

Justice must therefore organize the purposes together through equality, proportionality, truth, restraint, repair, and governmental accountability. A state cannot claim justice while punishing the weak and protecting the powerful.

Government Itself Must Be Subject to Law

Moral reconstruction must include offenses committed by public authority. The state should punish corruption, torture, unlawful detention, police brutality, judicial manipulation, and theft of public wealth. A criminal system directed only toward private citizens is incomplete.

Officials should not possess sacred immunity. They should be removable, prosecutable, and subject to independent courts. Public order is not served by protecting unjust rulers. Equal citizenship must begin with one universal legal person whose protection does not depend upon religion, sex, ancestry, marital history, disability, or prior moral reputation.

187Mohammad Hashim Kamali, Maqasid al-Shariah Made Simple (London: International Institute of Islamic Thought, 2008); Kamali, Shariah Law: An Introduction (Oxford: Oneworld, 2008).

Different Institutions for Different Wrongs

Not every moral wrong belongs in criminal law. Civil law may address marital obligations, defamation, financial loss, custody, and compensation. Administrative law may regulate licensing, professional conduct, commerce, and public safety. Religious communities may establish voluntary standards concerning membership, leadership, ritual, teaching, and moral discipline, but internal authority must remain nonviolent and noncoercive, and a person must remain free to leave.

Education and social welfare are also legal institutions in the broader sense. Education cultivates respect for property, sexual responsibility, truthful speech, sobriety, civic participation, and religious understanding. Social welfare provides conditions in which lawful conduct is reasonably possible through food, shelter, medical care, education, and economic opportunity.

Four Governing Principles

The constructive framework rests upon four governing principles. First, minimum coercion: where a legitimate purpose can be achieved through a less coercive means, the state should choose it. Second, reversibility: punishment should preserve as much possibility of correction, appeal, release, rehabilitation, and compensation as public safety permits. Third, individualized responsibility: no person should be punished because of group identity, family status, political association, or inherited religion. Fourth, actual harm: criminal law should focus principally upon conduct that causes or seriously threatens harm to others.[188]

These principles return to one central claim: the state never acquires ownership of the human body, conscience, or personhood. It may restrain liberty for serious and lawful reasons. It may not treat a human being as a disposable object of moral display.

188International Covenant on Civil and Political Rights, arts. 6, 7, 14, 17, 18, 19, and 26; Gabriel, "Reforming Hudud Ordinances," constitutional and human-rights safeguards.

A Reconstructed Map of the Offenses

The constructive transformation may be stated directly. Theft should be answered through restitution, graduated penalties, prevention, and serious treatment of corruption. Ḥirāba should be reconstructed as precise offenses of murder, terrorism, kidnapping, armed robbery, and violent conspiracy, with secure restraint but no spectacle. Zinā should be removed from corporal criminal law where conduct is private and consensual, while the law strongly protects against rape, abuse, exploitation, and abandonment of responsibility.

Qadhf should become equal protection against defamation through correction, compensation, and proportionate sanction. Drinking should be addressed through public-health regulation, treatment, and punishment of harmful conduct rather than private religious disobedience. Baghy should be transformed into precise law against armed insurrection while peaceful opposition remains protected and reconciliation follows conflict. Ridda should be removed entirely from criminal law where belief change is peaceful, with prosecution reserved for independently proven violence or treason.

What Is Preserved and What Is Rejected

This approach preserves the seriousness of wrongdoing, protection of victims, social responsibility, accountability, moral education, juristic caution, and the ethical objectives associated with the tradition. It does not reduce Islam to private sentiment. It rejects only the claim that moral seriousness requires bodily destruction or coerced belief.

It rejects amputation, cross-amputation, flogging, stoning, crucifixion, execution for peaceful apostasy, unequal legal personhood, and the claim that modern state violence becomes divine by citation.

Some may regard this reconstruction as departure from Islamic law. It may instead represent a deeper fidelity to justice, mercy, protection, and human responsibility. Preserving punishments that defeat those purposes is not fidelity. It is formalism.

Conclusion

The movement beyond the classical punishments does not leave a moral emptiness. Property can be protected without amputation. Public security can be defended without crucifixion. Family responsibility can be preserved without stoning. Reputation can be restored without flogging. Reason can be protected without beating the addicted person. Political order can be maintained without sacralizing rulers. Faith can flourish without executing those who leave it.

The modern state should pursue justice through institutions that are equal, proportionate, restorative, accountable, and restrained. Religious communities should pursue moral formation through teaching, persuasion, repentance, compassion, and example. The two forms of authority need not be hostile. They must simply remain distinct where coercion begins.

The constructive argument can be condensed into one sentence:

> *Preserve the value, reconstruct the law, and relinquish the violence.*

The chapter does not end by abandoning the moral tradition. It ends by insisting that its purposes be rescued from punishments that no longer express justice.

Conclusion

Justice Without Sacralized Violence in the Name of Islamic Law

This study began with Aḥmad Fatḥī Bahnasi's Al-Ḥudūd fī al-Islām, a compact but revealing presentation of the classical Islamic penal order. Its value lies in its detail. Bahnasi records definitions, disputed conditions, evidentiary rules, exceptions, and disagreements among the schools concerning the number, manner, and scope of punishments. That detail makes critical examination possible. The closer the system is studied, the more difficult it becomes to describe the ḥudūd as a single, complete, and self-executing divine criminal code awaiting restoration by the modern state.

The punishments may be described as fixed, but the law that activates them is not. Before a hand can be amputated, human institutions must determine ownership, value, protected custody, necessity, debt, family access, legal capacity, and doubt. Before zinā can be punished, the law must define marriage, iḥṣān, confession, retraction, pregnancy, witness agreement, privacy, and the relationship between Qur'anic flogging and stoning. Comparable choices appear in qadhf, intoxication, rebellion, and apostasy. At every stage, interpretation, classification, legislation, evidence, and judicial judgment intervene.

Juristic disagreement is evidence of serious intellectual effort, but it also limits the state's claim to certainty. A modern government does not restore one uncontested law. It selects among a plural tradition and constructs a code. If it abolishes slavery-based distinctions, adopts modern citizenship, uses forensic evidence, and combines rules from different schools while preserving bodily punishments as immutable, it engages in selective restoration. The surrounding legal world is reconstructed while the violence alone is declared beyond change.

The problem is not confined to legislation. Popular religious advocacy can give a disputed legal interpretation a social authority greater than its jurisprudential certainty warrants. When believers are taught that questioning a punishment may amount to questioning God, silence can be mistaken for consensus and legal reform becomes difficult before any courtroom is reached. The freedom to distinguish revelation from human interpretation is therefore part of the constitutional and moral reform this study requires.

The classical procedural safeguards deserve respect. Doubt, coercion, necessity, privacy, confession, retraction, reconciliation, and victim rights often restrain punishment. Yet procedure cannot make an unjust offense or disproportionate sentence legitimate. A fair apostasy trial still punishes conscience. A reliable theft conviction cannot make amputation reversible. A procedurally correct stoning remains killing through collective bodily violence. Mercy should not remain a technical escape at the gate; it should become part of substantive law through proportionality, restoration, rehabilitation, and restraint.

The ḥudūd also establish a political relationship between the governing authority and the human body. Amputation leaves a permanent public record. Cross-amputation creates disability. Flogging stages pain as instruction. Stoning distributes death among participants. Crucifixion converts the body into a display of governmental triumph. Such punishment may produce fear, but fear of government is not respect for law. The moral authority of a state rests upon fairness, reliability, protection of victims, and disciplined limitation of its own power.

Human fallibility makes irreversibility especially dangerous. Witnesses err, confessions may be coerced, judges misunderstand, governments become corrupt, and interpretations change. A state may release a wrongfully imprisoned person and compensate partially for lost liberty. It cannot restore an amputated hand or return life after execution. Institutional humility therefore requires the state to avoid punishments that no later justice can repair.

The modern state can magnify these dangers. It is centralized, bureaucratic, technologically capable, and intrusive. Surveillance, digital records, national databases, forensic laboratories, intelligence agencies, and mass communication can make rules developed under conditions of limited state reach far more invasive. A president is not automatically an imam, a parliament does not become divine authority by quoting jurists, and a police officer does not acquire sacred power through enforcement. The modern state's punishments remain human acts and must be justified as human acts.

Apostasy reveals the ultimate limit of governmental competence. The state may judge violence, theft, threats, or fraud. It cannot know whether faith is genuine, doubt has become disbelief, repentance is sincere, or how God judges the soul. It may compel a declaration, but it cannot compel belief. A profession of faith made under threat of death proves only the power of the threat.

Moving beyond the classical punishments does not require abandoning moral seriousness. Property can be protected through restitution, compensation, graduated sentencing, prevention, and punishment of corruption. Public safety can be defended through precise laws against murder, terrorism, kidnapping, and armed robbery, together with secure restraint rather than spectacle. Family responsibility can be strengthened through laws against rape, abuse, trafficking, exploitation, and abandonment, without stoning consenting adults. Reputation can be restored through correction, retraction, compensation, and proportionate remedies. Addiction and intoxication-related harm can be addressed through public health, treatment, licensing, and impaired-driving laws. Political order can be constitutional rather than sacredly attached to rulers. Faith can be taught, defended, and freely embraced without executing those who leave it.

The development from procedural reform to substantive transformation is not a rejection of the earlier scholarly journey; it is its continuation. The effort began by asking how enforcement could be made safer and more constitutional. Closer examination produced a deeper conclusion: where the offense violates conscience, where the punishment destroys bodily integrity, or where government sacralizes its own coercive choice, the state must relinquish the power itself.

The classical jurists should not be caricatured. They worked within their historical world and developed doctrines of doubt, necessity, reconciliation, and restraint. Respect for their intellectual labor, however, does not require permanent submission to every conclusion. They exercised judgment in their time. The present generation must exercise judgment in its own. A mature tradition can distinguish historical inheritance, moral objective, and present legal obligation.

The conclusion of this study is direct:

> *Modern states should abolish the classical corporal, capital, political, and conscience-based ḥudūd punishments.*

This does not require abandoning the moral purposes associated with them. It requires rescuing those purposes from state violence. Justice should protect victims, punish actual harm, preserve equal citizenship, respect conscience, maintain the possibility of correction, and hold government itself accountable. A state that mutilates a poor thief while protecting officials who steal public wealth has inverted justice. A state that punishes private morality while tolerating rape or domestic abuse has inverted morality. A state that executes an apostate while silencing scholarship has not defended faith.

The governing principle is equally simple:

> Preserve the value, reconstruct the law, and relinquish the violence.

Justice does not require the state to imitate every punishment of the past. It requires the state to protect human beings, restrain its own power, and accept full responsibility for the law it chooses to enforce. A government should never claim divine certainty for its human violence; a judge should never hide moral responsibility behind juristic selection; and the human body and conscience should never become the property of the state. It is the path toward justice without allowing any state, regime, or armed movement claiming to enforce Islamic criminal law to sanctify its own violence in the name of God.

Bibliography

Aḥmad Fatḥī Bahnasi. Al-Ḥudūd fī al-Islām. Shuʿāʿ al-Islām no. 12. Alexandria: Muʾassasat Shabāb al-Jāmiʿa, n.d.

ʿAbd al-Khāliq, ʿAbd al-Raḥmān. Wujūb Taṭbīq al-Ḥudūd al-Sharʿiyya. 2nd ed. Kuwait: Maktabat Ibn Taymiyyah, 1984.

Gabriel, Mark A. "Reforming Hudud Ordinances to Reconcile Islamic Criminal Law with International Human Rights Law." PhD diss., University of Cape Town, 2016.

Hallaq, Wael B. Shariʿa: Theory, Practice, Transformations. Cambridge: Cambridge University Press, 2009.

Hallaq, Wael B. The Impossible State: Islam, Politics, and Modernity's Moral Predicament. New York: Columbia University Press, 2013.

International Covenant on Civil and Political Rights. 999 U.N.T.S. 171. Adopted December 16, 1966.

Kamali, Mohammad Hashim. Freedom of Expression in Islam. Cambridge: Islamic Texts Society, 1997.

Kamali, Mohammad Hashim. Maqasid al-Shariah Made Simple. London: International Institute of Islamic Thought, 2008.

Kamali, Mohammad Hashim. Shariʿah Law: An Introduction. Oxford: Oneworld, 2008.